6/94

The Hispanic Experience
in North America

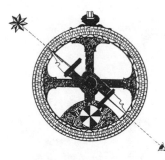

The Hispanic Experience in North America

Sources for Study in the United States

Edited by
Lawrence A. Clayton

Ohio State University Press
Columbus

*The preparation of this volume was made possible in part by a grant
from the Division of Research Programs
of the National Endowment for the Humanities,
an independent federal agency.*

CHRISTOPHER
COLUMBUS

50✝☆

QUINCENTENARY
JUBILEE

OFFICIAL QUINCENTENARY PROJECT

LIBRARY OF CONGRESS CATALOGING-IN-PUBLICATION DATA

The Hispanic experience in North America : sources for study in the
United States / edited by Lawrence A. Clayton.
   p. cm.
   Includes bibliographical references and index.
   ISBN 0-8142-0568-2
   1. Spaniards—United States—History—Archival resources.
2. United States—Discovery and exploration—Spanish—Archival
resources.   3. Florida—History—To 1821—Archival resources.
4. Southwest, New—History—To 1848—Archival resources.
I. Clayton, Lawrence A.
E184.S7H57 1992
973'.0461—dc20   91-39274
                                                        CIP

Text and jacket design by Kachergis Book Design.
Type set in Galliard by Connell-Zeko Type & Graphics, Kansas City, MO.
Printed by Braun-Brumfield, Ann Arbor, MI.

9 8 7 6 5 4 3 2 1

Contents

Acknowledgments

Three organizations were instrumental in initiating and organizing the conference that led to this book: the American Historical Association, the National Endowment for the Humanities, and the Library of Congress. I am especially grateful to three individuals—Dr. James B. Gardner, Dr. Richard Ekman, and Dr. John R. Hébert of those three organizations, respectively—for proposing, initiating, funding, and helping to organize the conference and the subsequent publication of its proceedings, this book. And of course I am immensely indebted to all the contributors to this volume, who gathered in Washington, D.C., in September 1987 to give of their time and experience. It goes without saying—but I'll say it anyhow—that this volume dedicated to the better understanding of our country's history and origins is the sum of their collective goodwill, effort, and expert knowledge.

Introduction

A contributor to this book, Eugene Lyon, aptly described his article as "a short summary of a lengthy topic." That description could serve just as well to describe this full work, which proposes to do nothing more than lead the reader into the field of the Hispanic experience in the United States. We have narrowed the scope of the subject by focusing only on archives and records for the study of that experience, and delimited it even more by surveying only those manuscript and other primary records that deal with the period 1492–1850.

All the essays that follow were read at a conference held in the Library of Congress in September 1987. The conference was dedicated to the subject of records for studying the Hispanic experience in the United States. It was prompted by several factors, perhaps the most important being the ongoing commemoration of the Columbus Quincentenary.

The year 1992 will mark the five hundredth anniversary of the voyage of Christopher Columbus. The great mariner, although Genoese by birth, sailed in the service of Spain, and his discovery is intimately associated with those Spanish sovereigns, Isabelle of Castille and Ferdinand of Aragon, who sponsored his voyage.

Columbus opened up vistas of a New World heretofore unknown to Europeans, and Spanish gentlemen and not-so-gentle men streamed across the Atlantic in the following decades to conquer and populate the islands and mainlands of this New World. Having subdued Hispaniola early on, the conquistadors soon rippled out to include Cuba and Puerto Rico in the small but growing Spanish Empire in America. By 1519 the mighty Hernando Cortés had launched his assault on the Aztecs of Mexico, and in 1532 Francisco Pizarro struck into the Inca Empire of Peru.

The story of conquest and subjugation in this New World setting is largely the story of Hispanic peoples. Although other Europeans such as the Portuguese, French, and English approached the New World as well, the sixteenth century belonged to Spain. Just as the Spain of the Hapsburgs dominated Europe and the Mediterranean, Spanish conquistadors dominated the Americas. From the centers of conquest in the Caribbean, Mexico, and

Peru, outriders spun the web of Spanish dominion into the remoter areas of the Americas, to places such as Chile and Nicaragua, and north from Cuba and Mexico into what the Spanish called Tierra Incognita del Norte and La Florida. It is this phase of the Spanish conquest and settlement of the New World that interests us, for La Florida and Tierra Incognita were terms used to describe the lands that would later become part of the United States.

The study of Spain in North America began to interest American scholars in the nineteenth century when parts of the former Spanish Empire were incorporated into the present-day boundaries of the United States by either treaty or war. With the new territories—such as Florida, Louisiana, Texas, New Mexico, Arizona, and California—came new people. Indians, Hispanics, blacks, mestizos, mulattoes, and others passed into American citizenship. They also carried a long history into the United States, a history of European conquest and occupation that predated the first permanent English and French settlements in North America.

Americans wakened to this different, somewhat mysterious and dark history that stretched from the medieval Moorish kingdom of Granada in Spain to the Pacific waters of California. In the nineteenth century Washington Irving wrote about the Moors in his *Tales of the Alhambra* while William Prescott produced his classic studies of the conquests of Mexico and Peru. Others in the twentieth century, none more prolific or with greater impact than Herbert Bolton, focused on what they called "the borderlands," or those territories that formed the northern fringes of the Spanish Empire in North America.

Bolton and his students, who fanned out from Texas and California, went to the original documents—many in Spain and Mexico—to discover with enthusiasm and delight the historical legacy of Spain in North America. The missionaries came alive and the great conquistadors of North America—Hernando de Soto, Francisco Coronado, Alvar Núñez Cabeza de Vaca—once again marched through the marshes of Georgia and deserts of New Mexico, this time into the pages of American history.

In the second half of the twentieth century, the Bolton enthusiasm for unearthing the glories of Spain faded, and borderlands studies settled into a rather quiescent period. Yet a new excitement has awakened scholars and laymen alike in the past three decades. Anthropologists and historians have come together to explore the interaction of European and native American peoples, each borrowing freely from the other discipline. The chapter by

Charles Hudson on "Research in the Eastern Spanish Borderlands" tells how this exciting and fruitful search has evolved in the Southeast.

Historians have in the past half-century gone beyond the old military-political-dynastic mode of writing history to making in-depth probes of the social, economic, cultural, and even geographic matrix of a people's history. This felicitous trend spilled over into borderlands studies as well and complemented the growing ecumenism of anthropologists and historians. What was life like on the frontier in New Mexico after the great battles were fought, the cities founded? How did the missionaries of Upper Sonora and Arizona first cultivate the friendship of the Indians, and then inculcate the values of Christianity and Spanish civilization? What did the settlers of St. Augustine eat in the eighteenth century? New questions are being asked, and new answers are being suggested as scholars probe more deeply.

Furthermore, new techniques are rapidly being developed to facilitate research. Microfilm was the boon of the first half of the twentieth century. Computer technology is revolutionizing our approach to document preservation and dissemination as we near the end of the century. The language itself is freighted with jargon: optical disks, laser beams, digitization, RAM, ROM, and the now notorious bites and bytes of computerese. Using the newest technology, IBM of Spain, the Fundación Ramón Areces, and the Ministry of Culture are now copying over nine million pages from the Archive of the Indies in Seville to optical disks. Take the archive home in your knapsack. John Kessel's whimsical-serious "Research on the Western Spanish Borderlands" takes a look at this futuristic landscape.

Finally, the Columbus Quincentennial has promoted all the above trends and more by catalyzing the interest of Americans in their past. Scholars have especially been provoked to look more deeply and widely into our Western heritage that dates not from Jamestown but from the age of Columbus, when Europeans first saw the United States. As the Western heritage is probed, increasing interest in the native Americans has become manifest, and some institutions, such as the University of Florida, have focused closely on how Europeans and Indians mixed and influenced each other. The Institute for Early Contact Period Studies is described by Michael Gannon in his "Documents of the Spanish Southeast Borderlands at the University of Florida." This institute has provided some of the most exciting finds in the history and archaeology of sixteenth-century America over the past few years. Douglas E. Jones reports on how the State of Alabama followed the trail of

Hernando de Soto in "Alabama and the De Soto Expedition," bringing to light a part of the southeastern past that lay buried in shadows and myth for almost five hundred years.

Each new encounter with the past, each new revelation has served to heighten interest and set new goals for scholars, librarians, and archivists alike, sometimes acting apart, more often together as providers get together with users to determine needs, methods, and priorities. One great problem, albeit a creative problem, has arisen amid this enthusiasm for studying, analyzing, and restoring the Hispanic past to North American history: the documentation available has grown immensely for the researcher, and it has grown unwieldy and even awesome. Why? David Buisseret of the Newberry Library offered one suggestion when he commented at the September 1987 meeting that U.S. historians have a "curious drive to photocopy or carry away the archive they are working on abroad," a comment that provoked some laughter. After it died down, Buisseret asked, "Is there anything in Spain we would not like to copy?" This drive to copy has produced in the United Stated thousands of rolls of microfilm of Spanish and Mexican archives, and we simply have little grasp of where it all is and what it all contains. Another conferee, Patricia Galloway of the Mississippi State Archives, stated the task succinctly: "Get control of what we have and make it available." To which Michael Riley of Ohio State struck the same chord with a different gong: "Let's get our Louis in order."

Thus, one of the principal goals of the conference in September 1987 was to address the problem of how to manage the documentation. Where are the documents? In what form? What are the contents? What access is there? Many of the answers to these questions are provided in part 1 of this book entitled "Archives."

Parts 2 and 3, entitled "Research" and "Projects," respectively, undertake to describe some ways in which modern scholars have both gathered and used borderlands documentation. The tales of running down documents is sometimes more exciting than the discovery itself, and these chapters reveal the directions different individuals and institutions have taken in studying the Hispanic presence in North America.

Part 4 is sure to be dated, for it reports on the fast-breaking technological breakthroughs related to the copying, preservation, and retrieval of documents. We include it to gently remind the reader who may still be dozing in the soft light of old and quiet archives, unchanging over the centuries, that the space age has intruded into those sacred, recondite corners of our world.

We think the news is exciting, even while we remember the dwindling winter light of a cold Sevillan afternoon, quietly handcopying a few words and sentences at a time onto our small note pad from the great dusty *legajo* (bundle of documents) in front of us.

The final part is entitled "Recommendations," and, in a sense, is the capstone of this book, for it both summarizes and projects. It consists of one chapter by John Jay TePaske of Duke University and the formal recommendations of the conference. Among these recommendations was the preparation of a guide to Latin American source materials in the United States. That guide is now being prepared, and its completion is but the next stage in our deeper and more profound understanding of the Hispanic experience in the Americas. The conference that led to this book was the initialing step, and we trust the reader will benefit and enjoy its contents as those of us did who gathered early in the fall of 1987 to consider a part of our past that has grown and continues to grow as we approach the twenty-first century.

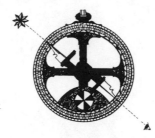

1 · Archives

Introduction to Part I

Laura Gutiérrez-Witt and Guadalupe Jiménez-Codinach are scholars trained in history, library science, and archival preservation. In their respective articles, they look both backward and forward. As historians, Gutiérrez-Witt and Jiménez-Codinach review the state of manuscript collections in the United States related to Spain and its empire in America and then suggest paths to better collection, identification, and dissemination. Gutiérrez-Witt provides us with a overview of collections in the United States and how many came into being, while Jiménez-Codinach details the current effort by the Library of Congress to identify and publish a major new finding aid to copies (largely microfilm copies) already in U.S. collections.

Michael Gannon tells us how Florida has pioneered in many instances the identification and collection of rich manuscript resources for the history of Spanish Florida and the Caribbean region. As is the case across the old Spanish borderlands, those states with a rich Hispanic heritage—the corolla of states from Florida to California—have taken the lead in collecting and making available the documents of their Hispanic past. Florida has been especially active with its Institute of Early Contact Period Studies in the past few years, and Gannon has been at the center of those activities.

Gene Lyon describes what he calls the "little used" archives of Spain—those small, often private collections that contain surprising treasures not available in the great public depositories such as the General Archive of the Indies. Lyon's report is one of the investigative historian, whose work is—like detective work—tedious and exhaustive. But it can lead to thrilling discoveries, and Lyon's creative, persistent searches have led to a deepening of our Hispanic cultural heritage.

Harriet Ostroff and Alan Virta describe the founding and evolution of the most important national effort to identify and make information available on our national manuscript treasures: the National Union Catalog of Manuscript Collections (NUCMC). This model program has evolved over the years, constantly attempting to maintain uniformity, to work in a comprehensive fashion, and to keep up with the rapidly advancing technological revolution brought on by the computer age. It is, at this time, the single best source for information on Hispanic and Latin American manuscripts and collections in the United States and, as such, provides us with a basis for future work on a comprehensive guide to Latin American manuscripts in the United States. But, as Virta so fittingly points out, the NUCMC descriptions are very brief, often ignoring vast amounts of information in collections. He argues persuasively for the creation of a major and unique guide to Hispanic and Latin American manuscript collections.

Pedro González was asked to perform perhaps an impossible task: review for the conference the holdings in Spain that deal with North America. The resources of Spain are vast and profound, and González succeeded admirably in providing us with this eagle's eye view.

LAURA GUTIÉRREZ-WITT

1. The State of Spanish Manuscript Collections in the United States

Spanish manuscript collections in the United States are numerous and varied, generally secure and well-preserved but more often than not incompletely cataloged, poorly identified, and therefore abysmally unknown and inaccessible. I believe this for several reasons, among them documentation or lack thereof, experience, hearsay, and intuition.

Definitions

The term *Spanish manuscripts,* as used in the context of this paper, refers to extant original archives (official records) or manuscripts (personal papers) that were created or gathered by Spanish civil and religious officials, organizations, or private individuals during the period from 1492 to 1850 in those geographic areas that now comprise the continental United States of America. Manuscripts that relate to these areas and are found in U.S. repositories, though created elsewhere, are also included in this definition.

Individual manuscripts may have naturally become part of a group of similar records, or similar records may have later been gathered into an artificial collection. Excluded from consideration therefore are Spanish manuscript collections in the United States that may deal with other geographic areas of the Americas as well as manuscript materials created by U.S. Hispanics after 1850, another large group of unknown and largely uncollected materials.

Creation of Manuscripts and of Collections

The availability of a number of directories, inventory guides, bibliographic compilations, and descriptions of individual collections and repositories indicates that Spanish manuscripts in the United States are numerous and varied. The Spanish manuscripts and the collections of them presently in the United States came into being in various ways. In defining Spanish manuscripts above, I referred specifically to original records created or gathered by Spanish civic and religious officials, organizations, or private individuals from 1492 to 1850 within the United States. The manuscripts, if created by either civil or religious representatives in the course of governance or administration, are defined as official records or archives. The official civil manuscripts were comprised of administrative or financial documents such as *ordenes, cédulas* (decrees), *residencias, visitas, relaciones, informes;* legal records such as *peticiones, demandas, testamentos, ventas, títulos, registros, poderes;* and military orders. The official church records, on the other hand, consisted of letters, *padrones,* informes, relaciones, and *libros de registro* (or registers of baptisms, marriages, and burials). If the documents were created by private individuals, the documents are defined as personal papers and can include correspondence, diaries, bills, daybooks, receipts, or other personal notes or items.

In certain instances, collections were naturally created, as when the accumulation of individual manuscripts grew out of the function of a certain office or agency. Some of these collections are still in existence and, surprisingly, have remained at or near their places of origin. Well-known examples are the Bexar Archives from San Antonio now in Austin, the Laredo Archives now in San Antonio, and the New Mexico Archives in Santa Fe. These collections are composed of records created in the course of governing a province, district, or town. In many cases these official records remained with government agencies well into the twentieth century. Other collections, such as the Louisiana Papers at the Bancroft Library in California, wandered about as political conditions changed and now are far removed from their place of origin. The 900 items in this collection were obtained by Hubert H. Bancroft from Alphonse Pinart, who had acquired the materials in Havana. Originally, the documents, correspondence of the governors of Spanish Louisiana and West Florida from 1764 to 1809, were probably located in governmental archives in these states during the Spanish period.[1]

Although some of these collections of official records were subjected to less than tender loving care in the past, today the materials for the most part are well cared for and reasonably secure, either in state archives or in academic manuscript repositories. A classic example is the case of the Laredo Archives, which were rescued from the trash bin by an amateur historian in

1934. Years later the City of Laredo decided to reclaim these papers although they were on deposit at St. Mary's University in San Antonio. Ownership reverted to the Laredo Historical Society, but the materials continue to reside in San Antonio for lack of a suitable repository in Laredo.

In many instances, manuscripts or collections of manuscripts migrated from Spain, Mexico, or the lands in question to the libraries of collectors—Adolph Sutro, James Lenox, Edward E. Ayer, Joaquín García Icazbalceta come to mind—and thence to renowned repositories of research materials. Found in many public and private libraries and archives, these artificially created collections are basically miscellaneous collections or diverse examples of "indiferentes generales," gathered by private collectors, often piece by piece and then donated to or acquired by the repositories. Actually, many of the better-known collections found in research repositories were created in this fashion.

Other collections were created artificially for a specific purpose. The volumes of correspondence by Franciscan friars held by the Chancery Archives of San Francisco are a case in point; these letters were not originally addressed to the archbishop. Rather, these personal letters of early missionaries were gathered years after their creation by a collector and subsequently donated to the Chancery Archives. Nonetheless, these materials document activities of Catholic missionaries working in the archdiocese from 1769 to 1840 and are properly part of the official church documentation of the archdiocese. On the other hand, the Chancery Archives of Los Angeles is comprised of mission registers, again official records, from various diocesan sites because correspondence from missionaries working in southern California is scarce. In the words of the archivist, "Southern California's early prelates were far too busy making history to care about recording it."[2]

There are probably as many variants of artificial collections created for specific purposes as there are collections. All collections are created with a specific purpose in mind, even if this purpose is simply the joy of owning such documentation.

The geographic area covered by these collections is astonishingly broad; discovery, exploration, and settlement of much territory in many states, not only in the Southwest, are the subjects covered by this documentation. States on the southeastern seaboard, in the Gulf Coast area, in the Midwest, and in the Pacific Northwest, as well as the Southwest, comprise the lands where conquest, exploration, and settlements sponsored by the Spanish Crown occurred. Until recently, the topic was little explored in a number of states. One discernible effect of the Columbus Quincentenary preparations has been the reclamation of the Hispanic past in many states where not only the general public but also many scholars were previously oblivious to or uninterested in this aspect of their history.

Identification of Collections and Repositories

Despite a number of efforts through the years to identify and inventory both collections and repositories, it remains difficult to ascertain the exact number of repositories that hold collections of Spanish manuscripts in the United States. I will, however, briefly review some of the projects and publications of the last eighty years that have attempted such surveys.

In 1889 the Act of Incorporation of the American Historical Association (AHA) cited "the collection and preservation of historical manuscripts" as one of its goals. Accordingly, its Public Archives Commission began surveying public archival repositories in the various states. By 1909 the AHA had published in its annual proceedings 41 surveys of 30 states, a number of which cited the presence of Spanish documentation. By 1912 the commission considered its work largely accomplished with 48 reports done and only a few surveys remaining unpublished. An interesting example of one of these surveys was the one of Alabama archives compiled by Thomas M. Owen and published by the AHA in 1904. Owen commented that "the civil records for colonial times at Mobile . . . are embraced in about 40 neat packages. . . . There are a few French papers, mainly land grants, and less English, while the great mass of them are Spanish."[3]

Another typical survey was that of the Archives of New Mexico, which listed the records found in eight territorial offices and five selected county seats. The surveyor also looked at seven church archives, but commented that lack of time and money precluded his examining "a rich mass of documentary material in the hands of private individuals who are descended from early Spanish and English settlers."[4]

The next survey of historical manuscripts in the United States occurred from 1936 to 1941, when the Historical Records Survey was organized and directed by Luther H. Evans. The national survey began as a federally funded project but reverted to state sponsorship in 1939. A preliminary survey of 100 entries describing repositories rather than collections was published in 1938, and Evans commented that 650 responses had been received from repositories that were to be included in the forthcoming state guides. At the request of the AHA Committee on Historical Guide Materials, ultimately the survey was to publish not only the state guides but also guides to manuscript collections and inventories of individual collections. Only 19 publications appeared before the outbreak of World War II.[5]

In 1961 there appeared what is still the most cited directory to manuscript collections, *A Guide to Archives and Manuscripts in the United States,* edited by Philip M. Hamer for the U.S. National Historical Publications Commission. The Hamer guide listed "the archival and manuscript holdings of some 1300 depositories in the 50 states of the United States, the District of Columbia, Puerto Rico, and the Canal Zone." Libraries, historical societies, museums, archival agencies, and other organizations were listed with information received via questionnaires and also from published guides, lists, directories, and other sources examined by the guide staff.[6]

About the same time, efforts to identify Latin American manuscript resources began in several countries as a result of discussions and decisions reached by the International Council of Archives in 1959. In the United States, a national commission was organized to develop plans to undertake a survey of Latin American manuscript collections and to publish a guide to those collections. Initiated in 1963, the project was based at the Institute of Latin American Studies, University of Texas at Austin. Although Gunnar Mendoza and his staff worked on the project for three years, the survey was not completed and subsequent efforts to resurrect it failed. Nonetheless, the preliminary list of collections compiled by Mendoza and his staff included 5,373 entries, and the index to repositories listed 450 institutions. It is unlikely that all these institutions hold Spanish manuscripts relevant to our discussion, but these figures do narrow the field down from Hamer's 1,300 repositories.

The publication of the *National Union Catalog of Manuscript Collections* (NUCMC) by the Library of Congress beginning in 1962 demonstrated anew the vastness of manuscript resources in the United States. The first volume of NUCMC for the years 1959, 1960, and 1961 listed 7,300 collections in 400 repositories, a number that closely approximates Hamer's findings.[7]

In addition to these broad surveys and projects, specialized directories and bibliographies have also provided either descriptions of collections and repositories or a bibliography of sources of information on them. I will briefly note several of the more relevant titles.

Although its scope encompasses Spain, Portugal, and Latin America, as well as Florida, Texas, the Southwest, and California, the *Handbook of His-*

panic Source Materials and Research Organizations in the United States by Ronald Hilton continues to be a useful source for locating Spanish manuscript collections. Hilton's inclusion of missions, museums, historical societies, public, private, and academic libraries, and government agencies in this guide made this compilation one of the more comprehensive sources for locating Hispanic materials. Hilton's 1956 survey described the holdings of 199 repositories of Hispanic materials.[8]

A somewhat later compilation by Russell H. Bartley and Stuart L. Wagner listed 107 archives, libraries, and special collections with holdings, both manuscript and printed, of Latin American scholarly interest. This guide also described numerous institutions in Canada, Latin America, Europe, and elsewhere. Compiled from published sources, the volume included an extensive bibliography of these sources.[9]

One of the most recent specialized guides to archives and manuscript collections of the Southwest, however, is *Spanish and Mexican Records of the American Southwest* by Henry Putney Beers. Published in 1979, the guide represents years of work by Beers in determining which repositories hold the early records of the four southwestern states: Texas, New Mexico, Arizona, and California. In the course of describing the records, Beers cited 121 repositories in the United States and 65 abroad. He did include some repository collections consisting solely of microfilm or photocopies of records held elsewhere.[10]

Individual repository guides and catalogs published as findings aids are yet another source for determining the number of Spanish manuscript collections in the United States. Some examples are the guides to manuscript collections at the Library of Congress, Yale University, the University of Texas, and the Newberry Library. All too often, however, published guides are available for only the major and relatively well-known repositories. Established institutions such as the Huntington and the Bancroft libraries also publish their own journals and/or exhibition catalogs. Hence, for the large or already well-known institutions, information on their varied holdings is easily found. Nevertheless, it remains an onerous task to attempt a complete census of the Spanish manuscripts at these institutions because it requires consulting innumerable sources.

The vast majority of manuscript repositories, however, produce only in-house lists or inventories, and other than occasional articles or notes in regional publications, their holdings are largely unremarked by the scholarly world. In this respect, regional historical publications perform a very important function: that of publicizing the holdings of these smaller repositories. Journals such as *Louisiana History, Mississippi Valley Historical Review, Southwestern Historical Quarterly, Florida Historical Society Quarterly,* the *Historical Society of Southern California Quarterly,* and *New Mexico Historical Review* often include articles highlighting specific collections or mention acquisitions of important archival materials by regional repositories. Identifying Spanish manuscript collections by this method is again a time-consuming task.

Categories and Location of Repositories

The repositories holding Spanish manuscript collections are of many types and scattered over a wide geographic area. Most of the repositories are associated with public and private academic institutions that support many of the most important manuscript repositories in the United States. The research necessities of academic life have created strong collections: the Bancroft Library at California, the Benson Collection at Texas, and the Beinecke Library at Yale, among others, hold Spanish manuscripts relevant for the purposes here.

Government agencies, particularly state archival institutions, also hold significant groups of materials. The New Mexico and the Texas state archives are notable examples. In Texas and in California, the State General Land Offices also retain relevant documentation. Other public agencies, such as libraries, also serve as repositories for Spanish manuscripts. A number of independent libraries such as the Newberry Library, the John Carter Brown Library, and the Huntington Library hold important collections of Spanish manuscripts as well.

It is probably the religious archives, however, that are the least known and least used. Catholic chancery archives in a number of states own documentation created by missionaries or parish priests within the diocese specifically for the bishop, or more likely, documentation that was gathered after the bishopric was established, an event that generally took place many years after the arrival of missionaries.

The selective perusal of guides and articles of repositories and collections that I undertook found repositories in seventeen states. Although much of the documentation is located in the Southwest, large bodies of materials are located in institutions in the Gulf Coast states as well as those from the District of Columbia eastward.

Physical State of Spanish Manuscript Collections in the United States

The well-known collections are for the most part secure and in good physical condition. The high quality of early papers and inks have, of course, helped to preserve these materials. It has been natural or man-made disasters that have damaged and destroyed some documentation. The 1909 "Preliminary Report on the Archives of New Mexico" presented by John H. Vaughan to the American Historical Association cited the destruction of the New Mexico records for 1598-1680 during the Pueblo uprising of the latter year. In 1870, later New Mexico records were sold by the American governor of the territory to the merchants of Santa Fe as wrapping paper.[11] Early California archives were destroyed during the San Francisco earthquake and fire of 1906, as was part of the Sutro Library.[12] Even as late as 1934 the Laredo Archives for the Spanish and Mexican periods, as I have mentioned, were almost thrown out of the district clerk's office in order to make room for newer records!

Recent national forums to develop preservation strategies for books represent an important initiative in which many manuscript repositories will also be included. Some concern must be raised, however, for those small repositories, often museums of local historical societies, that may not be able to afford trained staff acquainted with even minimal conservation techniques such as the use of acid-free paper and storage containers, environmental controls, and acceptable light-exposure levels for materials. Their collections of original manuscripts are probably fairly small, but valuable individual manuscripts are included and need to be preserved.

Microfilming—or other new techniques for preserving textual images—of these resources for preservation purposes seems to be an attractive alternative. In fact, a number of the larger collections are already available on microfilm. But these preservation alternatives are dependent on knowledge of available resources and their location. Frankly, I am not so sure that we have identified every extant collection, a point that brings me to my last topic, that of access.

The Question of Access

Unknown materials are basically inaccessible. All the numerous compilations and projects I have cited have been attempts to identify as many resources as possible. Yet none of them is truly exhaustive or complete. The task is simply too monumental to be accomplished by a single compiler or even a single group of individuals. Meanwhile, scholarly access to Spanish manuscript resources continues to be dependent on one or another scholarly network: the formal publication network that provides citations of items and collections used, or the informal one of hearsay or indirect reference. An enormous chasm continues to face scholars trying to locate Spanish manuscripts in the United States relevant to United States history. The best sources at present are the Beers compilation and the *National Union Catalog of Manuscript Collections*. But these do not cite every collection. Beers covers only four states, and NUCMC is heavily dependent on contributions from the repositories themselves. The repositories are often unable to contribute descriptions because their collections are not adequately cataloged. Most repositories have only minimal staffing, and the personnel they do have must often spend more time assisting users rather than processing and describing collections.

The projected on-line access of the NUCMC data base may improve access to information on the Spanish collections in the United States. Improved subject access to the NUCMC collections—which we hope the on-line searching capability will provide—will surely be a boon for scholars. The national bibliographic data bases, Research Libraries Information Network (RLIN) and Online Computer Library Center (OCLC), are also moving in the direction of collection-level cataloging of manuscript collections, and this policy will also improve access in the future.

Truly improved access will come about, however, only if enough repositories contribute to these data bases. It is time to think again of state, regional, or even discrete repository surveys whereby collection descriptions would be solicited or collected for inclusion in one or more national data bases. Printed guides still have a place in the scholarly world, but it is foolish not to avail ourselves of new technology if this can serve to accelerate the basic descriptive work that remains to be done.

During the course of this conference, descriptions of several projects already under way will be presented, the ARL Recon Project and the North American Program for Coordinated Retrospective Conversion, among them, and it behooves us to consider these as possible models for improved access to Spanish manuscript collections in the United States.

NOTES

1. Lawrence Kinnaird, ed., "Spain in the Mississippi Valley, 1765–1794," *Annual Report of the American Historical Association for the Year 1945,* (Washington, DC: GPO, 1949), p. xiii.

2. Francis J. Weber, "The Los Angeles Chancery Archives," *The Americas* 21 (April 1965): 410.

3. Thomas M. Owen, "Alabama Archives," *Annual Report of the American Historical Association for the Year 1904,* (Washington, DC: GPO, 1905), p. 528.

4. John H. Vaughan, "A Preliminary Report on the Archives of New Mexico," *Annual Report of the American Historical Association for the Year 1909,* (Washington, D.C.: GPO, 1911), p. 490.

5. U.S. Historical Records Survey, *Guide to Depositories of Manuscript Collections in the United States* (Columbus, OH, 1938).

6. Philip M. Hamer, ed., *A Guide to Archives and Manuscripts in the United States* (New Haven: Yale University Press for U.S. National Historical Publications Commission, 1961).

7. U.S. Library of Congress, *The National Union Catalog of Manuscript Collections, 1959/61–1984* (Washington, DC, 1962–86).

8. Ronald Hilton, *Handbook of Hispanic Source Materials and Research Organizations in the United States* (Stanford: Stanford University Press, 1956).

9. Russell H. Bartley and Stuart L. Wagner, *Latin America in Basic Historical Collections: A Working Guide* (Stanford: Hoover Institution Press, 1972).

10. Henry Putney Beers, *Spanish and Mexican Records of the American Southwest: A Bibliographical Guide to Archive and Manuscript Sources* (Tucson: University of Arizona Press, 1979).

11. Vaughan, *AHA Annual Report . . . 1909,* pp. 469–70.

12. Richard H. Dillon, "The Sutro Library," *News Notes of California Libraries* 51 (April 1956): 344.

GUADALUPE JIMÉNEZ-CODINACH

2. Spain's Archival Materials Available in United States Institutions

The Library of Congress Survey of Photographic Reproductions

It is rather fitting that the Library of Congress should have hosted a conference entitled "Archives and Records for Studying the Hispanic Experience in the United States, 1492–1850." The Library acts as the national repository for the United States in the tradition of the well-known bibliotecas nacionales in Paris, Madrid, México, Buenos Aires, Manila, and elsewhere. The Library has pioneered by itself, or in the company of scholarly organizations, many projects related to the focal objective of this conference: to produce a specific set of guidelines and recommendations for copying Hispanic materials abroad related to the study of the Hispanic experience in the United States. For example, more than 47 years ago on June 5 and 6, 1940, another group of scholars met at the Library for a "Conference on Microcopying Research Materials in Foreign Depositories." At this meeting Dr. France Scholes, then at the Carnegie Institution, suggested that in order to avoid duplication in filming documents in Spain, it had become essential to "have a general list of materials already available in the major collections in the U.S., particularly the Library of Congress, the Newberry Library, the Bancroft Library, the New York Public Library, the New Mexico Library, and others."[1] Thus the topic of this preliminary report comes to fulfill Professor Scholes's wish. His recommendations to the 1940 conference are still valid for all of us. "The greater effort should be made to pool our present resources to better advantage than in the past. The list of materials in major collections in this country mentioned above will not only be essential for any sane program but it will also help to make known what is already available."[2]

Another participant, Watson Davies from the American Documentation

Institution, posed a question still unanswered today: "Has anyone checked the Spanish archives copied in part by the Library of Congress' Project A to see what was destroyed in the Spanish [Civil] War and now exists only in microfilm in the Library of Congress?"[3] Davies was referring to what was perhaps the first systematic project ever attempted in foreign archives to gather photographic copies of valuable documents relevant to the history of the United States. Project Rockefeller, or Project A, was sponsored by a grant from John D. Rockefeller, Jr., for five years (1927–32), which was later extended to 1934.[4]

According to J. Rubin, the earliest microfilming done for the Library of Congress was produced in France in April 1928.[5] Regarding the Spanish archives, the Library installed cameras in the Real Academic de la Historia, the Archivo Histórico Nacional in Madrid, and two others, the Archivo General de Simancas, Valladolid, and the Archivo General de Indias in Seville.[6]

As early as February 13, 1929, the Library of Congress prepared a "Memorandum of Instruction for Preparation of Manuscripts for Photostats and for the Photostating, Indexing and Shipment of Facsimilies Therefrom." Each *legajo* (bundle of documents) had to be examined with a view to selecting the desirable materials for copying. However, the 1929 instructions were difficult to follow in places such as Spain. Professor Irving A. Leonard, working in the Archivo General de Indias (AGI) in 1930–31, recalls how he had to read under a lone, dim light bulb whenever electricity was available.[7] Blackouts, social unrest, and lack of appropriate equipment were common prior to and after the Spanish Civil War. Nevertheless, a substantial number of documents were copied. By 1947, 352,306 Spanish documents were reported copied under Project A.[8]

A second major conference on microfilms took place at the Library of Congress on December 27, 1948. The Conference on Latin American History (CLAH) of the American Historical Association and other participants were guests of the Library of Congress. A postwar atmosphere dictated its concerns. Spain and Spanish- and Portuguese-speaking nations were not as important in 1948 as they had been in 1940. The United States was becoming interested in other countries, particularly after the victory over the Japanese. As China, Burma, the Philippine islands, New Zealand, and parts of Europe rose in priority, Spain and Latin America fell. Likewise, the Library of Congress reexamined its policy toward microfilming. The effort now would be oriented toward the filming of newspapers in danger of deterioration or loss, the law collection, and materials not available in the United States, with emphasis on the "national history of the U.S." The Library of Congress thought it desirable, however, that other U.S. institutions with research interests should undertake filming abroad, for instance, the Bancroft Library on California-related materials. The Library of Congress continued its filming in France and England and contemplated a program in Mexico.[9]

A determining factor in the Library of Congress's decision to cease microfilming in Spain was the creation in 1950 of the Archivo Central de Microfilms by the Spanish government to make systematic reproductions of documents, manuscripts, and printed matter and to offer them to the public. In 1952 the Servicio Nacional de Microfilm was created and later the Centro Nacional de Conservación y Microfilmación Documental y Bibliografia (CECOMI).

Since the 1950s, the Library of Congress has bought some materials from the Centro, but it has not engaged in a systematic program of copying materials in Spain.

Notwithstanding the Library of Congress's pioneering work in foreign archives, its substantial number of microfilms and photocopies had never been catalogued in the manner of the Bancroft Library's holdings or those microfilms kept at Loyola University in New Orleans, for example. This lack of appropriate finding aids has made microfilms and photocopies an elusive tool of research, ever present but not fully available to scholars and institutions.

Aware of the unknown state of the quantity and quality of such materials, Spain's archival authorities and U.S. scholarly groups requested the Library of Congress to initiate a project that would "record the existence in American libraries of photocopies of materials from Spanish archives," in the hopes of alerting scholars to the availability of research material, thus avoiding expensive duplication and effort.[10] On February 9, 1987, the Hispanic Division of the Library of Congress began under my care the Archival Survey Project, or ASP, whose aims are stated as follows: (1) To survey photocopied holdings of Spanish archival documents relating to America—the Western Hemisphere—from the Archivo General de Indias (AGI) in Seville, the Archivo General de Simancas (AGS), the Archivo Histórico Nacional in Madrid (AHN), and other Spanish repositories found in research libraries providing public access in the United States; (2) To conduct the survey in two years and prepare for the publication of a guide or census of such holdings. (In reality, the ASP took three and a half years to complete the *Guide,* to be published in 1991); (3) To provide research organizations in the United States, Spain, and elsewhere with a more accurate assessment of holdings that currently exist, with the hope that a more rational approach for further copying may be adopted; and (4) To identify how and which documents had been copied in Spain and their availability to researchers in the United States, as well as the gaps to fill and the sections in the archives that have been recently micro-filmed, cataloged, numbered, and now are available for research.

To determine the best way to pursue this research project, some prelimi-nary steps were taken.

A bibliographical search made of works relevant to similar surveys and collections created in the past fifty years yielded 108 titles. Out of that num-ber, 50 main publications were reviewed. This search revealed that micro-forms (microfilm/microfiche), photographs, photocopies, and other mate-rial were seldom reported in such publications as the *National Union Catalog of Manuscript Collections*. Thus in 20 volumes, only 8 collections with these materials copied from Spain's archives were reported from 1959 to 1984. Ob-viously, institutions were not reporting on their photocopied holdings as carefully as they reported their original materials. Another common factor was the inconsistency in the way these materials were described. Most of the guides did not list the legajo number, others did not list the *sección* or *sub-sección* of the *archivo,* discrepancies occurred in the titles of the *secciones* or *ramos,* and so forth.

Since one of the most crucial factors for the successful outcome of a survey was an appropriate questionnaire, various drafts were tested at the Library of Congress's own Manuscript Division and Microform Reading Room. The first three drafts were found to be too detailed and difficult to answer, particularly by a repository with significant numbers of photorepro-duced materials. For example, the question whether the legajo at the archivo had been microfilmed in full could not be answered with the type of bib-liographic control available and the quantity of reels that would have to be checked by each responding institution. After six drafts and several revi-sions, a questionnaire was sent to over 215 institutions in June and July 1987.

All fifty states, the District of Columbia, Puerto Rico, the Virgin Islands, and Guam were covered. In each state and territory, repositories were chosen according to their holdings, that is, whether there were materials with some relation to Spain and its contribution to the New World.

While this institutional questionnaire was being drafted, another one was prepared for a selected number of scholars who had been either users or promoters of photoreproduction projects in Spain. More than 25 letters were sent to well-known researchers such as Professors Woodrow Borah, James A. Lewis, Mark A. Burkholder, John TePaske, David J. Bushnell, Michael Mathes, Jerry Cooney, Paul Hoffman, Stanley and Barbara Stein, Father Ernest J. Burrus, and Father Charles Polzer, to name but a few. Their responses and suggestions were carefully considered.

By December 11, 1987, the survey of institutions had received 156 replies, 40 of which reported photocopied material from Spanish archives in their collections, while 102 had no materials or were unable to answer the questionnaire for lack of bibliographic control or staff to organize it; two institutions have ceased to exist; 14 sent preliminary responses promising to send information soon; and 76 did not respond at all. (By late 1989 the results of ASP were as follows: of 270 institutions surveyed, 110 reported no materials, 49 institutions in 19 states plus Puerto Rico and Guam had this type of holding. In total the *Guide* will describe 53 collections).

Briefly, the responses show that there exists a substantial and valuable group of institutions that have gathered microfilms and other photoreproduced materials, mostly on a topic of research related to a geographical region, an institution, or a city. Collections with a definite, clear focus of research are the most common, perhaps reflecting the interests of individual scholars who started their own private collection of materials and later donated it to their academic institution, for example, Professor Lewis Hanke's materials found at the University of Massachusetts at Amherst, or the project begun in 1978 by Professors James A. Lewis and William L. Anderson to collect copies of Cherokee materials in foreign archives.[11]

Early Collecting

Perhaps the first photostats of the Dispatches of the Governor of Louisiana to the Captain General of Cuba (1766–1791) from the Papeles Procedentes de Cuba (31 volumes) were made as early as 1916 by the Carnegie Institution. Ten sets were distributed and have been reported in collections at Harvard and at the University of Illinois at Champaign-Urbana, while responses from other remaining institutions are no doubt forthcoming. It seems Papeles de Cuba, or PC, from the AGI have been the most popular ones to collect among U.S. institutions: P. K. Yonge Library at the University of Florida has 700 reels of them; Florida State University Library has 276 reels; Louisiana State University has 340 reels; the Historic New Orleans Collection and Loyola University of New Orleans have legajos 48–560 and

562–630; the Barker Texas History Center of the University of Texas at Austin and many others also hold microfilms or photocopies of various legajos. One must be cautious, however, when dealing with the Papeles de Cuba. There are approximately 2,375 legajos in the AGI section, of which most institutions in the United States have copied *only* from the one-third selected by Roscoe Hill in his *Descriptive Catalog of the Documents Relating to the History of the United States*.[12] Hill thought that only 928 legajos contained materials relating to the United States. Legajo 561 was missing and 8 were useless. Thus 1,447 legajos with materials from Veracruz, Castillo del Morro, Nuevo Reino de Granada, Santo Domingo, and other places were not thought to be pertinent to U.S. history. My research to date has shown that none of the following PC legajos has been copied in U.S. institutions:

Legajos	707–738	Cartagena de Indias
Legajos	739–757	Nuevo Reino de/Granada
Legajos	758–887	Costa Firme
Legajos	888–891	Santa Fe
Legajos	892–895	Veracruz
Legajos	896–915	Puerto Cabello
Legajos	916–920	Castillo del Morro
Legajos	924–1039	Cuba
Legajos	2270–2316	Puerto Cabello
Legajos	2347–2350	Capitanía General, Cuba

One should recall that the Papeles de Cuba cover the period 1761–1821 and an area that includes the Caribbean, the Floridas, Texas, New Spain, and the north coast of South America. How much of neutral trade, revolutionary movements, privateering, specie transactions, and other activities that involved U.S. ports and population with the Spanish American empire is not included in the U.S. collection?

A few preliminary observations can be made according to the responses received:

1. The three main archives in Spain, the AGI, AGS, and the AHN, remain the most copied by U.S. institutions. Nevertheless, other Spanish repositories, both regional and local, have also been searched for materials relating to the history of other countries as well as the United States. These repositories include the Archivo de la Corona de Aragón, the Archivo de los Condes de Revillagigedo in Madrid, the Real Academia de la Historia, the Archivo General del Ministerio de Asuntos Exteriores, the Archivo de No-

tarías, Madrid, the Servicio Geográfico del Ejército, and the Museo Naval, among others.

2. The institutional responses create several problems for the consistent presentation of my survey. There exist a variety of ways to identify the original document. For example, one response might use the 1929 classification of 14 *secciones* at the AGI, whereas other repositories that obtained their materials in a later period may use the 1977 division of 16 secciones. Confusion can be overwhelming if, for example, sección V is listed as Papeles de Simancas del Consejo de Indias y distintos Ministerios (1492–1856) in the 1929 fashion, or as Gobierno (1492–1854), as in the 1977 guide. Some collections have two sets of classifications from the AGI, the earlier one by *estante, cajón,* and *legajo;* thus, AGI, Gobierno, Audiencia de Guadalajara, legajo 586 could also be registered as Papeles de Simancas, 105-1-24. Furthermore, today the AGI has two more secciones: Tribunal de Cuentas (1851–1887), or XV, and Mapas, planos, dibujos y estampas (1519–1892), or XVI. In addition, the dates covering each sección have minor changes in relation to the earlier classification. Over the years, the different arrangements at the AGI have resulted in some misplaced documents. For example, under Gobierno, Audiencia de Méjico legajo 2761, there are some "Memoriales de pretendientes" not related to New Spain. Half of legajo 2734 is on Rio de la Plata and not on New Spain's missions. Some unexpected geographical areas are represented in the Audiencia de Guadalajara papers, for instance, the Presidio del Carmen (Campeche), 1770–1816.[13]

3. In addition to these internal variances at the AGI, the responses by U.S. institutions demonstrate other problems. Institutions with large collections have been unable to report accurately on the microfilming of each legajo for several reasons. One is the August 12, 1927, royal decree prohibiting the copying of full series at the Spanish archives. Some institutions that indeed had copied full legajos were reluctant to report them. In later years, when the prohibition was lifted, there were not enough staff and time to compare the microfilms with the existing guides to the legajos. In the most frequent case, institutions focused on a topic of research and selected materials from different sections and legajos while ignoring other documents. Or, as in the Library of Congress's microfilm projects from the 1920s to the 1940s, all printed materials in the legajos were excluded. As a result, today one is more apt to find incomplete legajos in microfilm-the exception being the full copy. This, as many scholars are aware of, is a handicap in the use of micro-

films and other copies. The person or institution that selected the materials according to its specific needs might have overlooked details interesting to another scholar contained in drafts, duplicates, printed papers, pamphlets, maps, drawings, and so on attached to a letter or a report.[14] Once a document is taken out of its context it becomes difficult to understand its individual history and meaning; or, as we say in Mexico, "Se reza el credo empezando por Pilatos," that is, "to recite the Creed starting with Pontius Pilate."

Nevertheless, even accepting the secondary and subsidiary nature of the photoreproduced materials and the natural desire of all scholars to work with the original documents, the fact is that some research projects must rely on microfilms and other copies from distant archives. Indeed, before new technological developments such as optical scanners and digitalization (see chapter 15) become household words, thus making obsolete earlier tools of research, it is still wise to appraise the location and availability of photoreproduced materials, not only because they have aided in preserving the original documents but because in some instances only microfilms or photographs may remain of an original group of documents lost or destroyed.[15]

It would not be surprising to find that the following eight legajos from Contaduria destroyed by fire at the AGI in 1924 exist somewhere as photostats in the United States:[16]

Consultado de Sevilla, Ordenación de las Cuentas de Avisos con sus duplicados, 1646–1649, 3-6-49/27.

Cuentas oficiales reales de Méjico, 10 de marzo a 15 de abril de 1760, 4-3-44/7.

Ibidem, 23 de abril de 1747 a 7 de mayo de 1748, 4-4-85/18.

Cuentas de Alcabalas, 8 de julio a 31 de diciembre de 1693, 4-6-135/8.

Relaciones de los encabezamientos y productos de Alcabalas, 10 de enero de 1680 a 31 de diciembre de 1700, 4-6-136/9.

Cuentas y Sumarios de Alcabalas de Méjico, Puebla y otros partidos (1719–1759), 4-6-137/10.

Testimonios de los Autores y Cuentas de los Tributos de Nuevas Leyes, 1629–1669, 4-6-148/21.

Cuentas, bastimentos, armas y municiones, 1597–1601, 5-6-10-12.

It would also not be surprising that the papers from the Audiencia de Quito, too deteriorated to be filmed, had been transcribed in the early years of this century by Father Pablo Pastells and now are available through microfilm at the Knights of Columbus Vatican Library of St. Louis University in St. Louis, Missouri.[17]

4. Conversely, several institutions duplicate the materials found in another one. For example, the France Scholes Collection at the Latin American Library of Tulane University, in part or in full, may be found in other repositories such as the Library of Congress and the Tozzer Library of Harvard University. The John P. Stetson Collection at the P. K. Yonge Library at the University of Florida, Gainesville, is also found at Louisiana State University in Baton Rouge, and so forth.

5. Finally, if we compare the expectations made clear through conversations, correspondence, and responses to the scholar's questionnaire, a visible gap is clear between the ideal guide for this sort of photoreproduced material as opposed to the possible guide that the Library of Congress had prepared.

Most users understandably have asked that such a guide provide the research scholars with the following information:

Provenance of a document—archivo, sección, or ramo, for example, of a legajo, *tomo,* or other form.

Whether all or part of each legajo, manuscript, etc. was fully copied, with enclosures, printed annexes, or other material.

Date, title, or other identification (sender, recipient) for each specific item; a thorough description of legajos and documents.

Geographic area covered.

When copying was done, and if and where other copies are available.

Condition of the microfilms and photocopies.

Availability of copies for a researcher, for example, interlibrary loan.

Listing of any local (U.S.) guides for the materials.

Good indexing of principal places and persons, and other subjects.

A preliminary appraisal of the institutional responses makes clear that some of these expectations cannot be fulfilled by the forthcoming guide. But it also tells us what is possible and within the realm of accuracy.

In my view, the survey and the *Guide* may be able to give us a publication with the following characteristics:

1. Clarity of information.

2. Systematic presentation of the entries in geographical, alphabetical, and institutional order.

3. Consistency, as much as it is possible in view of the different biblio-

graphic control, or the lack of it, used by the repositories in the reporting of the holdings in each of the nineteen states and the District of Columbia, Puerto Rico, and Guam.

4. Each entry divided according to the holdings copied from the three main archives in Spain (the AGI, AHN, and the AGS) plus other archives reported in alphabetical order and subdivided according to microforms (microfilm/microfiche), photographs, photocopies, and so forth.

5. The contents of each entry will be as complete as the response of each institution allows it to be. For instance, an asterisk may accompany only those legajos reported to be fully copied. Incomplete information may be discarded altogether but mentioned in footnotes or other supporting material.

6. The sheer numbers of legajos available (about 36,000 at the AGI alone), and the approximately 80 million documents within them, make it impossible to describe the content of each item; however, the researcher will have an organized picture of which legajos or items have been photoreproduced and which copies are available in the United States, or only through the archivo in Spain, or whenever possible, the Centro Nacional de Microfilm in Madrid. The scholar will be able to compare the number of legajos of each archivo and its general contents if he consults the pertinent catalog or guide available to that section's holdings, such as the AGI, Patronato Real. Thus, a comprehensive bibliographical segment will accompany the LC *Guide* as well as an index to its contents. Some 3,600 items have been listed in seven bibliographic sections of the *Guide*.

7. The Library of Congress *Guide* will be a useful tool for individual researchers as well as an aid to institutions interested in better analyzing the context of their holdings. It will be helpful to all institutions concerned with Hispanic culture in reviewing their photocopying policies. Some institutions may have found themselves with an assortment of copies related to various research seminars, scholars' projects, and donations that, as valuable as each may be, do not have any coherence or are in no way related to Hispanic original holdings at the institution. It is true that few research institutions have the necessary budget, or feel the need, to acquire complete legajos; the exception may be the Library of Congress and other public libraries that serve all kinds of interests and are not focused on a particular area or topic. It is also evident that others have done a wonderful job of building their collection around a specific theme, for instance, the Panton, Leslie and Company-related papers at the University of West Florida in Pensacola. Furthermore, some repositories have received by donation the papers

of a particular scholar that include photoreproduced materials, and they have neither the time nor the staff to prepare a finding aid. It can be argued that a fragmented collection or one selected to a particular individual's taste is of little general interest.

Although it is difficult to provide a formula for each case, general recommendations to institutions include the following:

1. Review your collections of original documents; check what is missing and photoreproduce the gaps if the original documents are available somewhere in the world. Because of the nature of Spanish imperial administration, duplicates, triplicates, and other contemporary copies may be available in distant places; what is incomplete in the AGI may be in better shape in Lima, Havana, or in Mexico City and vice versa. Indeed, some of the so-called contemporary copies may not be totally alike. Juan López Canceleda wrote in 1808 "If, even having it before us, in New Spain, we publish what we know not to be, . . . what distortions might have been made in the reports sent to the Junta of Sevilla by the Audiencia?"[18]

2. Survey your photoreproduced materials and compare your holdings with those in other repositories as soon as the Library of Congress *Guide* is completed. Perhaps some system of interlibrary loan and/or exchange program can be organized to complete a collection. For instance, all materials relevant to the history of an area could be donated to a specific library. In return, the receiving institution could donate material to another region. Copies may be made and exchanged among various libraries to share scarce resources, or to fund obtaining microfilms available at the Centro Nacional de Microfilm that can complete older copies.

3. If a repository owns original manuscripts with a rich bibliographical collection of an area topic or individual, it should try to obtain photoreproduced complete legajos in Spain or any other foreign archive related to the topic emphasized in your collection, for example, social, diplomatic, or economic history of America (the documents reported on here concern not only the Unites States but the entire Western Hemisphere), slave trade, women's history, children's history, demographic patterns, urban planning, independence movements, intellectual history, popular culture, and labor history. Slowly but surely one's research library will gather the tools, of both primary and secondary sources, needed for any project consistent with the topic. It is better to have a strong collection on a given topic than a myriad of fragmentary and incomplete materials.

4. University libraries or any other research repositories might pool the human resources offered by history departments in their area. History majors and graduate students should be encouraged to help catalog microfilms, photographs, and other materials and prepare finding aids for future use. The student will learn about the archival materials, cataloging techniques, and historical contents, and the institution will save staff hours and budget. History internships constitute perhaps one of the best exercises in the profession for future historians, as well as for future archivists and future librarians. Social science students could also profit from exposure to primary sources.

5. Once this present survey is completed and the *Guide* published by the Library of Congress, it will be important to continue publishing added entries as more repositories send information about their holdings. The *Guide* is but one step in a more comprehensive project that, if started with photoreproduced materials from Spanish archives, must one day report on other copies from other important archives, such as the Archivo General de la Nación in Mexico City.

6. Manuscripts are an endangered species, particularly as technological advances make them obsolete in the face of computer disks and other developments. Perhaps microfilms, microfiches, and other copies will also be replaced before we enter the twenty-first century. We are still responsible for their preservation as other generations before us preserved the contemporary copies we now find priceless.

NOTES

1. France Scholes, May 22, 1940, proposal in Library of Congress, Manuscript Division, Foreign Copying Program (hereinafter FCP), General Case File, 1901–40.

2. *Ibid.* Scholes suggested that if the ongoing war [World War II] made the execution of large-scale reproduction in other countries impossible, at least a concerted effort should be made to list U.S. research sources on Latin America.

3. "Letters of Robert H. Williams," May 27, 1940, LC, FCP, General Case File, 1901–40.

4. Grace G. Griffin, "Foreign-American History Manuscripts Copied in the Library of Congress," in *Journal of Documentary Reproduction* 3, no. 1 (March 1940): 3.

5. Jack Rubin, *A History of Micrographics in the First Person* (Baltimore, MD: National Micrographics Association, 1980), p. 55.

6. Griffin, op. cit., p. 6.

7. Personal interview with Professor Irving A. Leonard, April 17, 1987. Another handicap was the August 12, 1927, royal decree which stated: "Considerando que los modernos procedimientos de reproducción y copia en facsimile de documentos permite el traslado a países extraños de series enteras del venerado y rico tesoro documental que guardan nuestros Archivos, con tanta facilidad y escaso costo que de no poner cortapisa, condicionando las pretensiones de los investigadores, en cada uno de aquellos países extranjeros podría hacerse

la investigación del contenido de nuestros Archivos para desdoro y con daño del nuestro . . .
S.M. el Rey (q.D.g) se ha servido disponer: lo que queda prohibido en absoluto obtener
copias y fotocopias en serie de documentos existentes en los Archivos o en qualquiera otros
Establecimientos o Centros del Estado. Solo podrán concederse en casos excepcionales y de
Real Orden": Callejo, Madrid, August 12, 1927, in *Gaceta de Madrid,* no. 231 (August 19, 1927),
pp. 1030–31.

    8. "Microfilms in Project A," May 21, 1947, in Library of Congress, Manuscript
Division, FCP, General Case File, 1941–49.

    9. According to Leonor Ortiz Monasterio, director of the Archivo General de la Nación,
México, systematic microfilming at the AGN started in 1958. Photocopies had been made
since 1947. The AGN will soon publish *Fuentes para el estudio de México en los Estados Unidos de
Norteamérica y Canadá:* letter of Leonor Ortiz M. to author, July 1987.

    10. "The Columbus Quincentennial Observance in the Library of Congress. An Outline
and Prospectus," internal paper, p. 2.

    11. William L. Anderson and James A. Lewis, *A Guide to Cherokee Documents in Foreign
Archives* (Metuchen, NJ/London: Scarecrow Press, 1983). The authors explain their research
interest as follows: "As scholars doing research in our areas of specialization (England and
Latin America), we frequently come across large quantities of foreign materials on the
Cherokees that few scholars on the American Indian have consulted" (p. ix).

    12. (Washington, DC, 1916).

    13. Lino Gómez Candeo, *Los Archivos de la Historia de América,* 2 vols. (Mexico Distrito
Federal, Instituto Panamericano Para Geografia E Historia 1961), 1: 54, nos. 27, 26. One
scholar, Professor Jerry W. Cooney, has said that as a colonial "Paraguayanist," he has not
seen copies on this area. Perhaps the Library of Congress survey and the forthcoming *Guide*
may show that this area has not been neglected.

    14. E.g., the Seymour B. Liebman "Copies of archival materials related to the persecution
of Jews in Spanish America" in the Latin American Library at Tulane University.

    15. According to Abraham Peled, "The Next Computer Revolution," *Scientific American*
257, no. 4, (October 1987): 57. In less than fifty years computers have become essential to
industrial society; this technology will become an intellectual utility as popular as the
telephone. Workers at IBM research have developed a system capable of recognizing 20,000
words. Also, "a paper-like terminal allows the user to "write" on a flat, liquid-crystal
display; the computer recognizes the characters and translates them into commands, text or
drawings" (ibid., p. 62). One can only imagine all the changes this may bring to handwritten
documents.

    16. Listed in José Torres Revello's *El Archivo General de Indias, Sevilla: Historia y
Clasificación de sus Fondos* (Buenos Aires, 1929), p. 55.

    17. G. Jiménez-Codinach, "ASP Preliminary Report on Survey Replies," August 24,
1987, Hispanic Division, Library of Congress, pp. 4–5.

    18. Quoted in Verónica Zárate, "Juan López: Cancelada Vida y Obra" (Master's thesis,
National Autonomous University of Mexico, 1986), p. 163.

MICHAEL V. GANNON

3. Documents of the Spanish Southeast Borderlands at the University of Florida

Since 1954, when the University of Florida came into possession of the John B. Stetson Collection of 150,000 photostats of Spanish Florida materials from the Archivo General de Indias, the university's P. K. Yonge Library of Florida History has steadily expanded its collection of Southeast borderlands documents from Spain in photocopy form. The total collection numbers some 2.75 million document pages, most of which are accessible to researchers through finding guides and calendars developed by library chairperson Elizabeth Alexander and archivist Bruce S. Chappell.

Chronologically, the collection treats the two Spanish periods of Florida and the Southeast, 1513–1763 and 1784–1821. Geographically, the collection includes material from the Caribbean, the Florida peninsula and panhandle with their gobierno at St. Augustine and comandancia at Pensacola, the Gulf shore westward to the Mississippi, and the southeast interior lands of unsubjugated native Americans as far as the shifting boundaries of Anglo-American settlements in Carolina and Georgia. The documentation thus provides a picture not only of explorers, settlers, and missionaries of the early frontier but also of civil officials, populations, institutions, and social processes in a vast region of Spanish colonial hegemony or claims. Here, too, are glimpses of native chiefdoms and nations with which Spanish authority interacted, as well as of principal persons identified with English Georgia and Carolina, French Louisiana, Spanish Texas, and, of course, the Caribbean islands.

The library's borderlands holdings may be described under five headings: the Stetson Collection from AGI; the East Florida Papers; the Papeles Procedents de Cuba from AGI; recent first Spanish period acquisitions from AGI; and the also recently acquired Archivo de los Condes de Revillagigedo.

The Stetson Collection, made possible by a grant from hat maker John Batterson Stetson and drawn from the AGI, consists of 150,000 photostats of manuscript pages from 354 legajos. Photocopied by Irene A. Wright in the 1920s, they relate mainly to the first Spanish period, though some documents date as late as 1819. Unfortunately, the Stetson project, while selectively searching out Florida materials, did not film entire legajos. In recent years, as described on pages 37 and 38 under "first Spanish period materials," that deficiency is being corrected and we have now closed most of those holes as part of a new acquisitions program.

The Stetson Collection is a rich source of information about Spain's civil, economic, military, and ecclesiastical activities in Florida. The papers include correspondence between the governors and the king or Council of the Indies; correspondence between other local crown officials and government agencies in Spain: correspondence between the governors and other provincial officials, principally those in Havana, Santo Domingo, and New Spain; reports, with replies, from the secular clergy and from the Franciscan mission friars to the king and his council; and *expedientes,* which were collections of documents, mostly from legal cases, that yield important historical and sociological data about life in the borderlands.

Stetson also contains accounts of the many struggles that faced Spain's *peninsulares* (native-born Spaniards) and *criollos* (American-born Spaniards) in surviving the often hostile Florida environment, where they attempted to share the land with not always docile native populations, where fields were often barren, and where the English eventually made armed encroachments on them from Carolina and Georgia. The collection records the introduction of black slavery, the comforting growth and achievements of the Franciscan mission system, explorations, both seaborne and overland, of the American Southeast, and intermittent efforts to make Florida economically self-reliant. From many of these documents, too, one can compile data about native customs, languages, migrations, and population collapses. Altogether, Stetson is an abundant source, much of it still unused, for the student of borderlands history, ethnology, anthropology, geography, religion, or linguistics. The catalog cards that form the calendar for the collection number 14,000 and have been microfilmed on three reels, which are available through the P. K. Yonge Library.

Calendars have been prepared for this and two of the library's other collections. Each calendar is item specific for maximum archival accessibility. Each consists of a series of 3 × 5 catalog cards arranged chronologically. A card has three sections. The first contains the date of the document and its location within the collection. The second lists the place of origin, author, and if a letter, the addressee, the type of document, and length. The third is a brief summary in English of the contents noting topics covered and all personal and place-names.

The East Florida Papers is a collection on microfilm that dates from the second Spanish period, which began in 1784, when England yielded Florida back to Spain after a twenty-one-year interregnum, and ended in 1821 with transfer of sovereignty to the United States. During this period, Florida was divided into two provinces, one west with a capital at Pensacola, the other east with a capital at St. Augustine. The East Florida Papers, as they are called, constitute the official archive of the Spanish government of East Florida. The 65,000 documents comprising the collection contain approximately 250,000 pages. The original papers remained in St. Augustine after the United States took possession until 1869, when they were removed, first to Tallahassee and in 1905 to Washington, D.C., where they are housed in the Library of Congress. In 1965 they were microfilmed by the Roman Catholic Diocese of St. Augustine and returned to Florida on 178 reels. A calendar available on microfilm contains 56,000 cards. Also available on microfilm is a finding guide based on the LC inventory. This tool provides subject approach over a wide array of document sections. Like the Stetson, the East Florida collection has been relatively unused, despite the fact that it contains official correspondence with the Spanish departments of the time that governed the Indies: state, war, exchequer, grace, and justice. Also found here are correspondence exchanged with ministers and consuls of the United States; economic reports dealing with the English-owned trading house of Panton, Leslie and Company; and descriptions of Spanish relations with the indigenous populations of the interior, now almost entirely Seminole. Found out of context here, as is frequently the case in Spanish collections, is correspondence from Governor Manuel de Montiano in 1737–41. An index to royal decrees affecting Florida from 1595 to 1762 is also included.

By contrast there was no organized local collection that might be called the "West Florida Papers." Here the library has had to reconstruct on microfilm a West Florida archive from the **Papeles Procedentes de Cuba** in the AGI. These legajos contain documentation beginning in the early seventeenth century and are particularly rich for the northern rim of the Gulf of Mexico during the period circa 1760–1821. Using the descriptive catalogue of the Papeles prepared by Roscoe R. Hill in 1911–16 and thanks to the always generous cooperation of Doña Rosario Parra Cala, director of the AGI, the Florida library has amassed 761 microfilm reels of Florida material, all of which has been calendared. As I have explained elsewhere:

> Most correspondence of the period was first gathered into files (carpetas) accord-
> ing to types and levels of administration (civil or military, hospital, Indian rela-
> tions, ecclesiastical, etc.), after which the files were arranged chronologically and
> gathered into legajos, the time frame of which varied according to volume: some
> legajos contained correspondence for periods as short as four months, others for
> spans of twenty or more years. Although the correspondence conforms to the
> Spanish Royal Order (Buen Retiro, 21 August 1748) that limited each individual
> letter to a single subject, it is still an undertaking of some magnitude to locate that
> one letter a researcher is seeking without the calendar.[1]

This 60,000-card calendar is now available through the library.

It needs mentioning that the Papeles collection contains the Reales Cajas legajos of both East and West Florida during the second Spanish period, which constitute complete treasury records for the region. Here the Florida archival staff had to organize the legajos, foliating and arranging the docu-ments according to chronological and geographical criteria of the AGI, work that took approximately ten hours per legajo. It appeared that all the East Florida treasury accounts survived but that there were substantial gaps in the West Florida accounts. The library, in conjunction with the AGI and the Ministry of Culture, microfilmed all the Florida treasury records as such, but no warehouse, hospital, or other accounts, and published a microfilm edition, which is for sale through the Central Nacional de Microfilm in Madrid.

Recent acquisitions from the AGI have concentrated on **first Spanish period materials** not included in the Stetson Collection in the 1920s, when Irene Wright photographed selectively from the pertinent legajos. Thus we have filmed five reels of Florida materials in Patronato, a division of the AGI that contains key patrimonial, or sovereignty, documents for the Americas. In Contaduría, the archive of the Council of the Indies acting in its fiscal capacity, we have filmed thirty reels of Florida materials. In Contratación, the archive of New World commerce and taxes, we found enough previously unknown Florida documents to fill eleven reels. Each reel contains approx-imately 1,500 document pages.

Justicia and Escribanía de Camera, of course, contain the archive of the Council of the Indies in its judicial capacity ruling on civil and criminal cases in the Americas. These sections in later years contained the *residencias,* the records kept on the investigations routinely made into the affairs of each governorship upon its conclusion. Today these residencias often provide researchers the most useful overall view of a particular administration. With the acquisition of thirty-one reels of Justicia we now have all the residencias known to exist for the gobierno of St. Augustine in the first period.

Gobierno, which includes subsections pertinent to Florida—Audiencia de Santo Domingo and Audiencia de Mexico—constitutes section five of the AGI and originates with the Council of the Indies acting in its governmental capacity. The documents are arranged according to geographic region. Technically Florida should not be here because it did not report either to Santo Domingo or to Mexico but directly to the king or, as later, to the captains-general of Cuba. But Florida was included in these *audiencias* as a filing procedure and we now have forty reels of Florida documents from this collection.

In 1974 the AGI microfilmed all the manuscript inventories created by the AGI in the 1790s and early 1800s for Patronato, Contaduría, Contratación, and Justicia. The Florida library purchased all of them though they did not pertain exclusively to Florida, and they are available at Gainesville for researchers' use. Finally, notice should be taken of ten reels of material, mostly military for St. Augustine and Pensacola, that we have copied recently at Simancas and six reels of Papeles de Estado that we filmed at the Archivo Histórico National in Madrid.

The Archivo de Los Condes de Revillagigedo may well be the most important private archive brought to this country from Spain, dealing as it does with the founding of Spanish Florida, the extension of Spanish hegemony across the southern tier of states as far as and including California, and the administrations of two viceroys of Mexico. Of greatest interest to Florida historians is the massive documentation of the Revillagigedo family, of which Pedro Menéndez de Avilés and Pedro de Valdés—both intimately connected to the foundation of San Agustín—were the family's principal progenitors and precursors. The collection was first discovered by modern researchers in 1963 at Gijón in Asturias, and one bundle of the papers was microfilmed and brought to Florida at that time. The remainder of the documents, some 825,000 pages plus 167 color images and a reel of large charts, was microfilmed in 1985, under the day-by-day direction of historian Eugene Lyon, in a rented flat below a family member's apartment in Madrid where the papers are stored. The microfilming, co-sponsored by the St. Augustine Restoration Foundation and the Institute for Early Contact Period Studies, took six months and $230,000 to complete. Included in the 662 reels, now deposited in St. Augustine as well as in Gainesville, are 491 legajos; two large boxes of the *herencia* (inheritance) of the Menéndez family; four volumes of the residencia of the first viceroy of the family in 1757; four books of the account of "Ovideo y la Florida"; genealogical charts and royal titles; and *hijuelas*, or estate inventories. Here is an immense amount of material, virtually untouched, for book-length and monographic studies, dissertations and theses, and journal articles, not to mention corrective and additional data for already published works.

In 1982 the P. K. Yonge Library staff, working in Seville with existing guides and the original documents, completed a guide to all first Spanish period materials. Thus there now exists a systematic archival tool for locating and preparing lists of numbered legajos with the AGI sections that hold Southeast borderlands documents.

The library has created indexes to the photocopies in its possession of the Spanish transcriptions and other papers of late nineteenth- and early twentieth-century Spanish Southeast borderlands historians: those of Buckingham Smith stored in the New York Public Library, those of Woodbury Lowery and Jeannette Thurber Connor stored in the LC, and those of Joseph Byrne Lockey stored in the P. K. Yonge.

The acquisition of newly available published guides to the Archivo General de la Nación in Mexico has encouraged the archival staff to identify and to begin negotiations to microfilm important Florida documentation in that depository.

In 1985, following a visit to Havana, Cuba, by University of Florida researchers, the director of the Archivo Nacional, which operates under the Academia de Ciencias de Cuba, gave written permission to the university to copy the 2.5-million-page collection of *protocolos* documents in that archive. The protocolos collection includes notarial documents from the sixteenth through the eighteenth centuries. These, of course, are legal instruments such as wills, bills of sale, real estate transactions, and manumissions. The sixteenth-century papers have been transcribed, which is fortunate because nearly all the originals have disintegrated. The seventeenth- and eighteenth-century papers are in perilous condition and should be photocopied soon if they are to survive. The protocolos collection is important to Florida because it replicates in great part the notarial archive of St. Augustine that was lost to water damage and vandalism in 1812. It is also vital to the history of the entire Caribbean basin.

An exceptional offer of funding made to the Institute for Early Contact

Period Studies by a major Spanish corporation has set in motion several far-reaching acquisitions programs in Spain utilizing optional laser disk technology. Equipment now based in Madrid leads those of us who work with Spanish archival materials at the University of Florida to anticipate the development of significant new copying programs in both public and private archives in the madre patria that will relate not only to the Southeast borderlands but also to the Columbian voyages and to the first Spanish settlements in the circum-Caribbean.

NOTES

1. Michael V. Gannon, "Documents of the Spanish Florida Borderlands: A Calendaring Project at the University of Florida," *William and Mary Quarterly* 38, no. 4 (October 1981): 722.

EUGENE LYON

4. *Sources in Private and Little-Used Archives in Spain*

My topic deals with the "other archives" of Spain: that is, those other than the Archivo General de Indias, the Archivo Histórico Nacional, the Archivo General de Simancas, as well as other well-known state and institutional depositories, such as those of the Royal Academy of History, the Museo Naval, the Servico Histórico Militar, the Real Palacio, and the Escorial.

These other archives consist of private, ecclesiastical, notaries', municipal, university, and other institutional ones. Since there are scores of lesser archives in Spain, the space allotted here prohibits the full development of this topic. In any event, a mere listing of depositories with their general holdings would be of little use to any scholar. Individual investigators must follow their particular interest through existing general works on manuscript sources, make further selections through personal sleuthing, and then devote themselves to assiduous personal toil among the documents. The most that can be done here is to afford a glimpse at the characteristics and promise of some of these other archives through general discussion and the presentation of some potentially illustrative examples. I will confine myself to depositories with which I am personally acquainted or for which reliable observations exist.

As many scholars could testify, there are useful and valuable materials in lesser-known archives in Spain. Limiting oneself to the use of the major depositories could mean forgoing vital elements of a research topic, or missing important material that complements better-known sources. Consulting the other archives may also enable one to trace historic personages to their familial, property, ecclesiastical, and/or educational roots. Some of these depositories contain materials relevant to the territories within the present boundaries of the United States, offering the possibility of significant contributions to the disciplines of history, geography, anthropology, and the natural sciences.

In seeking paths through the maze of Spanish archives and libraries, some general source works may be quite helpful.[1] The cautions given by Ernest Burrus to verify in advance the current availability of particular depositories and prevailing working hours are even more relevant to the planning of work in small archives or libraries. Observation of the necessary courtesies in seeking permission from the proprietor or other authority should also be considered well in advance of the projected visit. The interested scholar may be able to obtain some detailed published guides before leaving the United States, thus aiding in the shaping of an efficient search. The final caution relates directly to the Archival Survey Project recently undertaken by the Library of Congress. The investigator should do the necessary homework to learn if material germane to the search already exists in a usable reproduction of the primary documentation in the United States.[2]

Most general guides, however, represent but someone's selection, possibly limited, of materials from a particular depository. The UNESCO guide, for example, contains useful references to areas now within the present United States. It does include many, if not all, depositories outside the major archives but does not pretend to furnish full indexes of the archives that it delineates. Rather it relies upon existing card indexes and published or unpublished guides.

What follows is a discussion of several types of Spanish depositories with some examples of the documentation they offer.

Notaries' Archives

A number of scholars, including Ruth Pike, James Lockhart, Antonio Muro Orejón, Louis-André Vigneras, Paul Hoffman, and Consuelo Varela, have worked with profit in the voluminous notaries' archives of various Spanish or Hispanic-American communities. They exist, in separate depositories or guarded within regional, municipal, or university archives, in all the regions of Spain.[3]

After the beginning of the sixteenth century, the notaries public of Castile were required to include in their records (*registros*), entire sworn documents (previously notes, or protocolos, had summarized legal acts). But the earlier name, protocolos, was retained. There had earlier been a duality of jurisdiction over these records, as the registros were considered the notaries' property, while government exercised a degree of control over their safe-keeping. In the early modern period, as the volume of these records became greatly amplified, notaries' societies and municipal authorities began to provide central archives for them. Later, royal orders provided that notaries licensed to practice at court should furnish their records to chosen conservators, and, in 1765, created the Madrid Notaries' Archive for that purpose.[4]

These rich depositories offer uncounted thousands of documents about the status of minors and adult persons, marriage and dower relations, the granting and cancellation of powers of attorney for many purposes, and a variety of other business and personal instruments. These include deeds of sale, ship freightings, testaments, letters of credit, loans, leases, mortgages, and labor and apprenticeship contracts. The sheer volume of all this paper is daunting, as the archives are organized around notaries' holdings (each separate notary's register comprised an *escribanía*). Since the cities often had a number of notaries, there may be many concurrent parallel series of escribanías. The materials were bound by year, each bundle usually containing an alphabetic index. In confronting this mass of documentation, teamwork would truly seem essential. In many locations, facilities for reproduction are unavailable.

In Cádiz, when this speaker first saw them in 1970, the notaries' records were in a parlous state. Stored in the municipal garage, a structure attached to the Puerta de la Tierra, many of the document bundles (legajos) were damp and rotting. They were jumbled on shelves without organization but obviously contained valuable materials from the early sixteenth century, many relating to the Indies trade. A first primitive index was followed by a more complete one made by Paul Hoffman. Now the records have been set aside in more adequate quarters and inventoried more fully. In Sanlúcar de Barrameda, the essential Archivo de Protocolos was destroyed by fire in 1923.

The Seville notaries' archives include some 17,000 protocolos in more than 21,000 books and bundles dating from 1441 and is housed in a former Dominican church on the calle Feria. It is distributed into twenty-four notaries' sections. Thus a seeker must follow a number of concurrent series for any particular year, each of which may have produced multiple bundles for each notary; hence the great volume of records. It is therefore useful to know or discover which particular notary or notaries may carry the documentation that is sought. Professor Hoffman's work is especially helpful here; he has isolated certain notaries whose work usually affected the Spanish Indies.[5]

Under the direction of Professor José María Ots Capdequí of the University of Seville, a team of five scholars, including Dr. Antonio Muro Orejón, undertook a major investigation of the Notaries' Archive of that city in the late 1920s and early 1930s. The four-volume work produced from their labors has been very helpful for students. It is, however, comprised of selected documents and is stronger for some sixteenth-century time periods than for others. As an example of this, Professor Paul E. Hoffman has located important documentation about the remarkable man named Lucas Vázquez de Ayllón and his North American exploration attempts.[6]

These notarial depositories are excellent sources for social, economic, and traditional narrative history. For our purposes, they contain records of early explorers and settlers within present U.S. borders. For example, key information about several of the sixteenth-century Florida Adelantados (those who received contracts from the crown to conquer and settle in Florida) comes from the notaries' archives of Seville, Cádiz, and Madrid. The Mahon (Baleares) notaries' archives have been consulted by linguists and historians working on the eighteenth-century Minorcan colony brought to British East Florida by Andrew Turnbull.

Accessibility to Spanish notaries' archives is fair to good, but working hours are often short. Some of these notaries' archives may now be found sheltered within regional provincial historical depositories, such as those in Oviedo, Santander, and Bilbao.

In sum, Professor Hoffman may have best described the notaries' archives when he termed them "the last truly rich source of historical information still awaiting study by students of the expansion."[7]

Chancillerías

There remain records of two chancillerías in Spain: at Valladolid and Granada. First, these were tribunals in civil and criminal matters and of appeal from their entire province. They also dealt with nobility cases and entailed estates. There was no appeal beyond them, except for rank injustice, or to the king in grave cases under heavy bond.

Because of the richness of material often found in legal cases, these archives should be sought out. Search for data about persons affiliated with Spanish colonial North America within present U.S. boundaries may be well rewarded there.

Private Archives

The most important archives for the history of the Americas are those of the dukes of Alba, Veragua, and Infantado, but there are many other private depositories of interest in Spain. Some have suffered losses due to the ravages of nature, war, and civil conflict; others have been otherwise destroyed, divided, or sold to private collectors. But some remain in sufficiently good condition to be very serviceable examples of their type. One of these is the Archive of the Counts of Revillagigedo, presently located in Madrid. They have recently been completely microfilmed by the St. Augustine Foundation in collaboration with the University of Florida, with copies deposited in the United States.[8]

The Revillagigedo archive contains a lengthy series of documents (in the case of one family, exceeding seven hundred years) of honors, entailed estates, inventories, wills, familial relationships, correspondence, and legal cases relating to the families whose records have become joined over many centuries. It therefore offers excellent opportunities for the study of land tenure, material culture, historical events, and biographic detail.

This archive relates to twenty-four major families and other minor affiliated ones. The outside observed dates of material are 1215–1967, but the heaviest concentration is from about 1450 to 1920. There are 491 legajos plus books of indexes, property inventory, accounts, large genealogical charts, and books of privileges (filmed in color). The filming yielded in excess of 850,000 pages on 662 reels of microfilm. The archive contains papers of many of the families involved in the Spanish Florida conquest led by Pedro Menéndez de Avilés (whose materials are in the Canalejas and other sections). A substantial part of the archive consists of the private—and many of the governmental—papers of the two counts of Revillagigedo who served as viceroys of New Spain. However, the material of importance for colonial Texas, California, Florida, and Louisiana in the archive goes beyond the time periods of their regimes.[9]

Professor James Lewis of Western Carolina University was kind enough to describe the location of another set of papers: those of Don José Solano y Bote, captain-general of the Armada and first Marqués del Socorro. Some of these, including materials about the siege of Pensacola in 1781, are to be found in the archive of the marquesses of Monsalud in Badajoz. Other parts of the Solano papers are in the records of the Conde del Carpio.[10]

The archives of the dukes of Medina-Sidonia have been divided, with some of the papers in the Archivo General de Simancas. A portion of the archive was located in SanLúcar de Barrameda, but at least some of the papers were reportedly exported from Spain and offered for sale.

A small but important private depository is that of the Instituto de Valencia de Don Juan. Founded in 1916 by the count of Balencia de Don Juan, the institute is located on Fortuny Street in Madrid. It holds a notable collection of medieval ceramics and other objects of art, a fine library, and an archive. This contains the records of the House of Altamira and contains many papers once the property of Mateo Vázquez, secretary to Philip II. The consultas from the Council of the Indies and correspondence to and from major sixteenth-century figures make this little depository of particular and concentrated value.[11]

University Archives

The Biblioteca Universitaria of the University of Seville offers but one example of fine manuscript collections available at Spanish universities. It contains the narrative of Fray Antonio de la Asención, "Relación breve en que se da noticia del descubrimiento que se hizo en la Nueva España en la mar del Sur desde el puerto de Acapulco hasta más adelante del Cabo Mendocino (19th century)."

Ecclesiastical Archives

A cluster of Spanish archives analogous to those of the notaries for number, volume, and difficulty of investigation are the records of individual church parishes. Those scholars who have utilized the Florida parish records or other similar depositories will affirm their value in demographic, economic, or biographic studies. It requires time and patience to follow an investigation in these scattered and often isolated records. Through Professor Hugo Ludeña we understand that the microfilming of a number of parish depositories in Extremadura is proceeding.

Tracing the Jesuit records for the Florida missions of 1566–72 involves the investigator in the Archivum Provinciae Toletanae Societatis Jesu, an important accretion of papers secreted in Belgium from 1931 until the end of the Spanish Civil War and now established in Alcalá de Henarea. Felix Zubillaga utilized these as his primary source for two volumes relating to the first

Florida Jesuit mission. They constitute excellent sources for the historian and the anthropologist.

Zubillaga notes the proved lacunae in the body of Florida Jesuit materials. Even though some materials were found in the Fondo Jesuitico at Rome, he located some of the Florida documents in the New Spain, Brazilian, or even Japanese sections of the Alcalá de Henares depository. A complex of Madrid depositories also contains Jesuit material, including large quantities in the Jesuitas section of the Archivo Histórico Nacional and in the Real Academia de la Historia. There is other documentation in a Jesuit depository in Loyola.[12] Efforts continue to find the remnant of the records of the Franciscan missions once existing in Spain but now largely lost.

An important depository is that of the Obispado de la Diócesis de Barbastro in northeastern Spain near Lérida. The documentation that came to rest there relates to the former bishop of the diocese, Iñigo Abbad y Lasierra. The bishop's papers, though clearly much reduced in volume from their original extent, contain much worthy of notice, including materials he used in his California and Florida histories.[13]

Miscellany

As mentioned above, the regional or provincial archives are most useful and may contain historical notaries' materials, ecclesiastical documents taken from those institutions by governmental authorities, or other important papers. These documents may display data about figures or events in Spanish times within our current national boundaries.[14]

Spanish municipal archives may hold valuable documentation for colonial America, including areas within the present United States. For example, the municipal archive of Mahón in the Balearic Islands has the original contract between Andrew Turnbull and his Minorcan colonists, written in 1768 before their transportation to East Florida.[15]

Summary and Conclusions

Documentation about the United States in colonial times may be found in a variety of lesser-known Spanish archives: private (familial and institutional), notarial, municipal, ecclesiastical, legal, university, and others. As an example of this dispersal, there appear to be at least thirty-four depositories in Spain that carry material of value for colonial Florida alone. Within archives, material about the present United States may be concentrated in coherent series or it may be widely scattered among other documentation.

Leaving these resources to be unearthed by random individual scholarship probably would mean that they would remain largely unused and unknown. On the other hand, dealing more fully with such a mass of diverse and scattered resources would require a systematic attack involving substantial commitments of funds and skilled personnel over time. The first obvious step would be to determine the extent of the pertinent materials already available in the United States; this implies correlation work in the United States and a wide-ranging survey in Spain. In archives where the pertinent materials do not appear in compact series but must be winnowed out of other voluminous documentation, the cost of the survey per se would be substantial.

Upon the completion of a survey, priorities would have to be set for the reproduction of materials considered the most important and/or endangered. It might be appropriate to consider the reproduction of elements or sections of those notaries' archives known to contain important documentation about the present United States: Cádiz, Seville, Madrid, Oviedo.

The location of individual documents within a particular depository and their preparation for transcription or reproduction require persons able to read the materials, select the relevant documents, and handle them properly. Time and training are needed to assemble fully qualified teams for the work. Since many smaller Spanish depositories furnish no adequate permanent duplication or filming services, arrangements would have to be made for that work. Such tasks can be fraught with difficulties and must be carefully planned.

In archives such as those of the notaries, note taking may not be cost effective and is always subject to inaccuracy. On the other hand, manual computer entry still requires the time for transcription or summarization of each relevant document, thus slowing the process. An alternative would seem to be complete microfilming and/or optical scanning of individual documents, pieces, bundles, or even whole sections known to contain significant portions of relevant material. Although newer technologies—such as manual computer entry, optical scanning, and laser disk storage—may supplement or replace microfilming, the labor-intensive aspect of any project—selecting and preparing the documents—remains.

In conclusion, I suggest that the "private and little-used archives of Spain" constitute a major and to some degree untapped resource for our history, one that would be costly and difficult to make fully available. The value of the documentation in enabling a greater knowledge of our Hispanic past may, however, well repay such an effort.

NOTES

1. General works that include at least some references to lesser-known Spanish archives are Ernest Burrus, "An Introduction to Bibliographic Tools in Spanish Archives and Manuscript Collections Relating to Hispanic America," *Hispanic American Historical Review* 35, no. 4 (November 1955): 443–83. See also Dirección General de Archivos y Bibliotecas, *Guía de Fuentes para la Historia de Ibero-América conservadas en España*, 2 vols. (Madrid: UNESCO and Consejo Internacional de Archivos, 1966–69). Another useful source is José Tudela de la Orden, *Los manuscritos de América en las bibliotecas de España* (Madrid: Ediciones Cultura Hispánica, 1954). An older but serviceable work is Roscoe R. Hill, *Fuentes para el estudio de América en los archivos españoles* (Washington, DC: Instituto Panamericano de Geografía e Historia, 1937); also *Guía de los archivos estatales Españoles: Guía del Investigador* (Madrid: Servicio de Publicaciones del Ministerio de Educación y Ciencia, 1977).

2. Burrus, op. cit., pp. 444–47. In order to examine printed works on different depositories, it may be well to consult a general bibliography on Spanish archives, such as that of Luis Sánchez Belda, *Bibliografía de los Archivos Españoles y de Archivística* (Madrid: Dirección de Archivos y Bibliotecas, 1963). The Commission for Educational Exchange between the United States of America and Spain has published a guide, "Libraries and Archives in Spain" (Madrid: n.d.), which itemizes a number of lesser-known Spanish archives. The several publications of "News from the Center for the Coordination of Foreign Manuscript Copying," published by the Manuscript Division of the Library of Congress, are helpful for their description of specific archives and listings of published materials relating to manuscript sources in them. Dr. Guadalupe Jiménez-Codinach is currently director of the Archival Survey Project of the Library of Congress.

3. There is a listing of notarial archives in Spain in the excellent work of José Bono, *Los Archivos Notariales* (Cuadernos de Archivo, 1. Sevilla: Consejería de Cultura de la Junta de Andalucía, 1985). See also Antonio Matilla Tascón, "Escribanos, notarios y Archivos de Protocolos en España, *Boletín*, Dirección General de Archivos y Bibliotecas 84-85 (July-October 1965): 16-26.

4. See Bono, *Los Archivos Notariales*, p. 13.

5. See Paul E. Hoffman, "The Archivo de Protocolos de Sevilla," *Itinerario* 5, no. 1 (1981): 39-45. Also, on the same topic, see Consuelo Gil Arrando, "Archivo de Protocolos, un testigo de la historia de Sevilla," *Sevilla* 92, no. 20 (October 1986): 60-62. See also Bono, *Los Archivos Notariales*, pp. 16-17.

6. The work produced by the Ots Capdequí group was published as Instituto Hispano-Cubano de Historia de América, *Catálogo de los fondos americanos de Archivo de Protocolos de Sevilla*, 4 vols. (Seville: Compañía Iberoamericana de Publicaciones, 1930-34). For many years, a *fichero* of the documents located by the study team also existed in the closed building of the Institute on the Plaza Cuba in Seville; its location is now unknown to this writer. Paul E. Hoffman describes some of the Vázquez Ayllón material in "Archivo de Protocolos de Sevilla." More detail will be found in Hoffman's *A New Andalucia and a Way to the Orient: The American Southeast during the Sixteenth Century* (Baton Rouge and London: Louisiana University Press, 1990).

7. Hoffman, "Archivo de Protocolos de Sevilla," p. 39.

8. Positive microfilm copies of the Archivo de los Condes de Revillagigedo may be found at the St. Augustine Foundation, 20 Valencia St., St. Augustine, FL, and at the P. K. Yonge Library of Florida History, University of Florida, Gainesville, FL.

9. See José María Patac de las Traviesas, S.J., *Guía del Archivo del Excmo. Sr. Conde de*

Revillagigedo, 4 vols. (Gijón, 1984). *Antiguos Indices,* 10 rolls, contain older manuscript indexes. These two indexes are on the microfilm. There also exists a modern unpublished index, 72 pp. by family, section, and microfilm roll number (St. Augustine Foundation, 1987). A detailed index is in preparation.

   10. Personal communication, Dr. James Lewis, Cullowhee, NC, 1987. See also José Luis Santaló Rodríguez de Viguri, Don José Solono y Bote: Primer Marqués del Socorro, Capitan General de la Armada (Madrid: Instituto Histórico de Marina, 1973).

   11. See, e.g., "Memoriales de adelantado Pedro Menéndez acerca de armadas y negocios de la Florida y Lanzarote, 1569-70," *Archivo del Instituto de Valencia de Don Juan* (hereinafter AIVDJ) *Consejo de Indias-Correspondencia,* Envío 25, H, nos. 161-68; this details the deliberations of the four main royal councils about Spanish Florida and the requisite beginning of the crown subsidy, and also contains revealing correspondence about the discontent of the Jesuit leaders about their Florida mission. This material, translated, is in the records of the St. Augustine Foundation, St. Augustine, Florida. Also of interest is "Relación de lo que el adelantado Pero Menéndez de Avilés había hecho en la pacificación de la provincia de la Florida, 1565," from AIVDA, Peru, Envío 48, no. 100. The archive should be fully studied for material from New Spain, Santo Domingo, Spain, and other sections relative to colonial North America. For some information about the archive, see *Guía de Fuentes* (UNESCO), 2:412-39. The royal secretary's material can be examined through comparison with some letters found in Carlos Riba García, *Correspondencia privada de Felipe II con su secretario Mateo Vázquez, 1567-1571* (Madrid: Consejo Superior de Investigaciones científicas, 1959).

   12. For an excellent discourse on the several Spanish Jesuit archives, see *Guía de Fuentes,* 1:565-66, n. 1. Felix Zubillaga discusses the lacunae and describes his extensive work in the Jesuit depositories in *Monumenta Antiquae Floridae: 1566-1572* (Rome: Monumenta Historica Societatis Iesu, 1946), 73*-75*, 91*-106*.

   13. See Marie Helmer, "Documentos americanistas en el Archivo de Barbastro," *Anuario de estudios Americanos"* (Seville: Escuela de Estudios Hispanoamericanos, 1951), 8:543-67. A more recent work that has utilized material contained in the archive is that of Sylvia Lyn Hilton, *Descripción de las costas de California* (Madrid: Consejo Superior de Investagaciones Ciéntificas, 1981). Iñigo Abbad y la Sierra's work on Florida is *Relación del descubrimiento, conquista y población de las provincias y costas de la Florida* (Madrid, 1785), published later by Manel Serrano y Sanz in *Documentos históricos de la Florida y Luisiana, siglos XVI at XVIII* (Madrid: Librería General de Victoriano Suárez, 1912-13).

   14. The Provincial Historical Archives of Spain are described in the UNESCO volume as well as in *Guía de los archivos estatales Españoles.*

   15. See *Guía de fuentes,* 1:284-85.

HARRIET OSTROFF

5. The National Union Catalog of Manuscript Collections

From the Printed Volume to On-Line Data Base

"The dream of scholars, librarians, archivists, and curators of manuscripts for more than a half century is being realized." That is the first sentence of an early progress report written by Lester Born, the first editor of the National Union Catalog of Manuscript Collections (NUCMC) in 1960.

Dreaming and planning must go on for a long time before a national project involving hundreds of people can actually come into existence. NUCMC is no exception to this pattern. As early as 1870 and again in 1896, historians and librarians discussed the need for a catalog listing manuscript collections. A genuine manuscripts union catalog movement did begin in 1939, when the American Historical Association established a Special Committee on Manuscripts. The committee's 1947 report contained a recommendation that a national register of manuscripts be established at the Library of Congress (LC), or other appropriate repository, with a budget of $250,000 for a three-year period. In 1948 that committee was abolished, to be replaced in 1949 by the Joint Committee on Manuscripts, formed by the Society of American Archivists and the American Association for State and Local History. In 1951, the Library of Congress representative on the joint committee wrote the chairman a letter proposing that a national register of historical manuscripts be created at LC as a subsidiary of its National Union Catalog project. This was to be accomplished in two steps: the formulation of rules for cataloging manuscript collections, and then the printing of LC cards for manuscript collections prepared from copy supplied by both LC and other repositories holding manuscript material. The cards would be available for sale, and eventually an annual supplement to the Library of Congress Author Catalog, with periodic cumulative volumes, would be published.

This is, in fact, what did happen. The Library's proposal was well received. Both the Joint Committee and the National Historical Publications Commission (NHPC) supported it and agreed to advise on the creation of what was then called the National Register of Manuscript Collections.

At this point, the Library of Congress faced the task of creating cataloging rules for manuscripts. In 1952, a committee, composed of both cataloging and custodial staff, was appointed. The members of the committee from the Library's Processing Department saw their assignment as further progress in providing cataloging rules for special materials. They considered it essential that catalog cards for manuscript collections be able to fit into a general library catalog and that any new rules should be in accordance with the accepted cataloging rules of the time—the American Library Association (ALA) Cataloging Rules for Author and Title Entries (1949) and the Rules for Descriptive Cataloging in the Library of Congress (1949)—and that the new rules be approved by the ALA. The members of the committee from the Library's Manuscript Division, who were not catalogers, understood the need for these requirements. They felt their primary role was to explain what kind of information needed to be provided for and leave it to the cataloging experts to find the appropriate way to do it. All members of the committee also knew that it was of great importance that the rules be acceptable to the repositories holding manuscript collections; without their cooperation there could be no national register.

For the next few years LC's Committee on Manuscript Cataloging, with the support of the ALA, worked on the rules. Members of the joint committee and the executive director of NHPC reviewed various versions of the drafts while copies of the rules were sent to manuscript specialists throughout the country. The responses were generally very favorable and in 1954 LC issued the Preprint of Rules for Collections of Manuscripts. Step one toward a national register of manuscript collections was accomplished.

During this same period LC and other interested groups also put their efforts into planning for the national register. The favorable responses to the rules also indicated a willingness by several large repositories to cooperate with the proposed national register. Francis L. Berkeley, Jr., indicated in his address, "History and Problems of the Controls of Manuscripts in the United States," given at the 1953 meeting of the American Philosophical Society, that effective control of unpublished source material required not only national scope but also regular cooperation between repositories and the staff of the register. Early efforts at LC (and later ones continuing to the present) were designed to attain that goal.

The original plans for a national register at LC called for the inclusion not only of collections of private papers of individuals, families, and organizations in repositories open to the public, but also of privately owned archives and collections at the local, state, and national levels. Moreover, it was considered desirable to include information about collections in Canada and Mexico and, eventually, in other foreign countries.

In 1954 LC's Union Catalog Division drafted some specific plans for establishing and maintaining a national register of manuscript collections. These included the following activities: (1) clipping, pasting, or typing entries from published guides and from the shelflist of collections in the Library's Manuscript Division (which had never cataloged their collections); (2) interfiling them in one alphabetical file; (3) compiling an index to that file; (4) looking for descriptions of additional collections in other publications; and (5) editing the copy sent by other cooperating institutions for inclusion in the file. Alternate plans for temporary typewritten entries giving the name, size, location, and citation to be published description were also proposed. These plans did not result in any immediate actions except to change the name of the proposed project to the National Union Catalog of Manuscript Collections. The question of whether special funds were needed to cover the initial cost of the project and what form the index to the manuscript collections should take remained unresolved.

During the next three years, in an effort to determine the editorial costs of compiling a national union catalog of manuscript collections, LC conducted studies and sent out questionnaires to ascertain the volume of work involved. In 1957 the Librarian of Congress called a meeting attended by LC staff members and representatives of the Society of American Archivists, American Historical Association, and others, at which it was decided that LC should take the initiative by applying for a grant to start the project.

The Council of Library Resources came through with a grant of $200,000 to LC in November 1958, and the NUCMC moved from being a proposal to an operational project. The money was to provide for (1) gathering the data; (2) editing the information and preparing catalog entries; (3) printing catalog cards, supplying them at no charge to the repositories that contributed the copy, and selling them to others; and (4) maintaining a dictionary card catalog at LC. The grant also provided financial support for an Advisory Committee on the National Union Catalog of Manuscript Collections to guide and encourage the undertaking. The immediate goal was to prepare uniform descriptions of circa 3,000 collections in the Library of Congress and another 24,000 in about 75 cooperating repositories. In May 1959, a section head, three catalogers, and a clerk typist were appointed to form the Manuscripts Section in the Library's Descriptive Cataloging Division and made responsible for compiling NUCMC.

By September 30, 1959, after only five months of existence, the section had received reports on circa 3,500 collections from eleven repositories and cataloged 825 collections, while cards were being printed regularly. Although NUCMC was now a reality, it differed somewhat from the original proposal. Because financing was limited, the scope was reduced. Only collections in repositories open to the public and located in the United States were eligible for inclusion. This eliminated material that was privately owned or in foreign repositories. Another significant exclusion was that of archival material, which was defined for NUCMC purposes as "the formal and informal records that are generated by the administrative, organizational, or operational activities of public bodies and private organizations, together with documents received or collected by them in connection with their activities," and remain with the institution that created them. However, archival material that is available to the public in a repository dissociated from the creating institution, and personal, professional, or nonfunctional material housed in archives are eligible for inclusion in NUCMC.

The definition of what constituted a collection was and remains somewhat ambiguous. The first information circular issued by the NUCMC staff defines a collection eligible for NUCMC as

> a large group of papers (manuscript or typescript, original, or copies, of letters, memoranda, diaries, accounts, log books, drafts, etc., including associated printed or near-print materials), usually having a common source and formed by or around an individual, a family, a corporate entity, or devoted to a single theme. Small groups consisting of a highly limited number of pieces should not be reported as collections in themselves but should be taken care of by more inclusive reports covering many such groups.

The practice of combining small collections for cataloging purposes in order to create NUCMC entries for artificial composite collections has remained somewhat controversial. However, this practice did make it possible for material that would otherwise be excluded to appear in NUCMC. Information Circular No. 1 was later revised to include the following statement:

> Collections generally consisting of one or more linear feet or of fifty or more items (either separate pieces, or bound or boxed together) will ordinarily be included in the NUCMC. Collections of lesser size, particularly those containing various kinds of records, or significant single items, such as diaries, journals, minute books, or ledgers, will be included when justified by the repository on such grounds as historical importance, research potential, or association value.

The use of the words *generally* and *ordinarily* and the option for inclusion of very small collections or single items under certain circumstances were designed to provide more flexibility in determining eligibility for NUCMC. Later information circulars offered additional guidelines for the inclusion of other kinds of materials such as oral history transcripts and photocopies or microforms when the originals were not in an American repository open to the public.

No money was initially alloted for the publication of a printed volume. When, after two years, it was apparent that scholars' needs could not be adequately served by a card catalog at LC, plans had to be made for the preparation of a published volume. The first two volumes of NUCMC, one for 1959–61, appearing in 1962, and the second for 1962 with indexes for 1959–62, appearing in 1964, were both issued by commercial publishers. All later volumes were published and distributed by the Library's Cataloging Distribution Service.

At the time NUCMC came into existence and for many years later, despite the limited surveys undertaken by LC and others, little was known about the actual number of manuscript collections in existence in the United States. It was generally thought that after a few years the bulk of manuscript material would already have been listed in NUCMC and the work could be continued by one cataloger taking care of the small trickle of reports flowing in on a current basis. This belief proved to be erroneous. The publication of *A Guide to Archives and Manuscripts in the United States* by the National Historical Publications Commission in 1961 provided much needed information about the availability of source material in the United States. Known as the first Hamer guide, it became a very valuable working tool for the NUCMC staff during the 1960s and early 1970s. Information in it was used as a basis for form letters to potential contributors to NUCMC. It also made clearly evident how much material had not yet been reported to NUCMC.

One of the basic policies laid down at the very beginning was that no travel to a potential contributing repository for the purpose of preparing descriptions of collections by NUCMC staff be permitted. While Council of Library Resources money did permit travel by the section head, such travel was only for the purpose of obtaining cooperation from repositories. The repositories themselves were required to prepare some form of description and submit it to the Manuscripts Section.

Contributions from repositories are by no means of equal quality or quantity. Some descriptions require considerably more work on the part of the NUCMC staff than others. Although the original proposal for a national register called for uniform descriptions, this has never been possible. Approximately half the information about manuscript collections is submitted to NUCMC on specially prepared data sheets. The rest is submitted in a variety of forms, including catalog cards, accession sheets, inventories, published guides, and in recent years, computer printouts. Even the information on data sheets is not uniform, and no amount of editing and research on the part of the NUCMC staff can make the resulting catalog entries completely uniform or consistent. The ability of repositories to respond to NUCMC staff queries is also unequal. An uneven product is the inevitable result of a work dependent on the contributions of many people with varying backgrounds and unequal resources.

After its initial grant in 1958, the Council of Library Resources made supplemental grants totaling another $170,565 to continue work on NUCMC to July 1964. After that, Congress appropriated enough funds to make the project part of the Library's work. This has continued to the present. Approximately 2,000 collections have been cataloged each year, and with only a few exceptions annual volumes have been published. The fourth volume of NUCMC, including 2,089 collections cataloged during 1986 and 1987, together with a separate index volume, was published in 1990. It brings the total number of collections cataloged to approximately 58,525 in 1,325 repositories. In addition to the 1986–87 index there are six prior cumulative indexes and a separate index to the 1985 volume.

During the long span of NUCMC's existence, many changes took place. Cataloging rules were revised at least twice. Attitudes toward many concepts and disciplines changed drastically in response to events. Policies and procedures for cataloging and indexing had to change accordingly. Therefore, there are marked differences between the early volumes and the later ones, particularly in the indexes.

Because NUCMC is only one of the many missions of the Library of Congress, it has to compete for a place among other priorities of the Library. Although NUCMC was not always given as high a priority as those who are primarily concerned with manuscript material may have wished, the Library has never abandoned its support. During the thirty-one years of NUCMC's existence, the Library has undergone many critical periods, involving not only fiscal crises but severe shortages of space and staff as well.

The size of the NUCMC staff and the resources allocated to it have varied over the years. Most of the time the professional staff consisted of a section head and three catalogers who were also indexers. It was usually not possible to increase the number of staff members as the work load grew, and the backlog of uncataloged collections and the length of time between receipt of data and appearance in a published volume increased accordingly. At the present time there are four full-time catalogers.

Being a federal agency, the Library was not able to benefit from what seemed to be the abundant grant money dispensed by the National Endowment for the Humanities and the National Historical Publications and Records Commission, especially in the 1970s. The fact that grants from these two agencies enabled manuscript repositories to improve control of their holdings and increase their reporting to NUCMC may be an important factor in the growth of the NUCMC backlog.

Technological advances during the 1960s, 1970s, and 1980s brought automation to the Library of Congress and other repositories. Of necessity, the requirements for automation procedures involving books were given top priority at LC. Only gradually was attention given to other forms of library materials such as maps, music, audiovisual material, and manuscripts. The list of projects requiring the attention of automation experts at the Library of Congress is very long and manuscripts were usually not at the top of any list. For a long time nothing could be done toward the automation of NUCMC.

NUCMC staff did participate in the development of plans for a format for the machine-readable cataloging of manuscript and archival materials, and NUCMC's needs were taken into account when the MARC AMC format was developed. Even though many others were able to utilize the AMC format and reap its benefits before the NUCMC, eventually this situation changed.

In 1985 the Library formed technical and management committees to plan for the automation of NUCMC, and by March 1988 the NUCMC staff began entering records catalogued during 1986 and 1987 into the Research Libraries

Information Network (RLIN). Since that time, descriptions have been entered on a current basis. As of September 1990, approximately 5,500 NUCMC entries were in RLIN.

The first fully automated issue of NUCMC—a combined volume for 1986 and 1987 with a separate index—was published in 1990 by the Library's Cataloging Distribution Service from MARC tapes produced by RLIN. The twenty-fifth NUCMC volume, 1988–89 and separate cumulated index for 1986–1989, will be published in 1991. MARC tapes for collections appearing in both issues are also available for sale by the Cataloging Distribution Service.

The 1985 issue of NUCMC was a transition between the manual production of the preceding 22 volumes and the 1986–87 volume, which was entirely computer produced. The 1985 volume was produced by using personal computers with much manual manipulation. Because its index was not cumulated with earlier indexes, its preparation provided the opportunity to make extensive changes in indexing policy in order to prepare for automation and the integration of NUCMC into a national on-line data base. Because NUCMC is no longer a stand-alone product, many modifications were necessary to better integrate with other records in the data base. Some of the changes made for 1985 were experimental and were modified again for the 1986–87 volume. Furthermore, since NUCMC will continue to exist in printed form, its compilers face the double challenge of meeting the needs of both on-line users and those who must rely on a published work. There are numerous difficulties in meeting such a challenge. Fortunately, the MARC AMC format has been widely accepted by repositories holding archival and manuscript materials, and the need for greater standardization is generally well recognized. The days of rugged individualism in the description of manuscript collections are over. The current acceptance of uniformity may make the task of compiling NUCMC somewhat easier in some respects than it has been. Perhaps repositories will be more willing to provide the level of information necessary to conform to national standards, resulting in a more useful product for everyone.

NUCMC information in both on-line and printed form will provide additional benefits to researchers. Those who do not have access to any on-line data base will eventually be able to read descriptions of manuscript collections that are now available only online. Those who do have access to an on-line data base will be able to find descriptions of collections in repositories that are not able to provide on-line entries on their own. There are many repositories that find it difficult or impossible to contribute to an on-line network. Those repositories will depend on the NUCMC staff to do it for them.

Those who are responsible for the compilation of NUCMC are well aware of the many difficulties inherent in changing from one system to another. It is inevitable that mistakes were made and delays occurred. However, with perserverance, such obstacles can be overcome, and eventually both the quality and quantity of descriptions in NUCMC will increase and access to them will improve.

ALAN VIRTA

6. *The National Union Catalog of Manuscript Collections and Hispanic Manuscripts*

Harriet Ostroff's chapter is a thorough account of the early history of the National Union Catalog of Manuscript Collections.[1] That history sheds much light on the proposed guide to Hispanic manuscripts in the United States. I will use Mrs. Ostroff's paper as a departure for some comments specifically directed toward NUCMC and its use by Hispanic scholars.

The National Union Catalog of Manuscript Collections was created at the Library of Congress in 1959 to make available to the scholarly world short descriptions of manuscript collections in American repositories. For the first five years NUCMC was funded by a grant from the Council on Library Resources; ever since it has been fully funded by Congress. In twenty-three volumes published since 1959, NUCMC has described approximately 56,000 collections in 1,300 repositories. All are indexed by names of persons, corporate bodies, and subjects. Regrettably there is no single unified cumulative index to NUCMC at present. From testimony of many graduate students, I know that searching long lists of names in the myriad of NUCMC indexes is a favorite research assignment of some senior professors.

Relief, however, will soon be on the way, at least for personal names. The British firm Chadwyck-Healey, Incorporated, has invested many hours of research and labor in compiling a unified name index to the first twenty-five years of NUCMC (1959–84).[2] This source certainly makes the searching of names in NUCMC a much easier task, something that even full professors will be able to do themselves. I am sorry to say, however, that there are no plans at present to create a unified index to the tens of thousands of corporate names or subject terms.

Among the 56,000 collections described in NUCMC are many related to Hispanic topics—from a capsule description of the Bexar Archives in Texas to descriptions of collections at the Hispanic Society in New York. Hispanic-related materials often turn up in unlikely places.

A few months ago I was cataloging a number of collections from the Bourne Historical Society in Massachusetts. Bourne Historical Society had never been listed in NUCMC before; it was not listed in the Hamer guide of 1961 or the NHPRC guide of 1978. As I thought about what to say at this conference, one of their collections came to mind, the papers of a man named Walter Gibbs Beal: four letterpress books dated 1874–85.

Representatives of the Bourne Historical Society told us that Mr. Beal was a railroad manager in Cuba for J. P. Morgan, and that these papers were letters he wrote from Cuba with information on sugar prices, crops, politics, and the conditions of workers on plantations. I remember wondering at the time if any Cuban scholars outside Bourne, Massachusetts, knew of the existence of these papers. If they are not well-known, once the next volume of NUCMC is published, the world of Cuban scholarship will be enriched at least in a small way. This is the value of NUCMC and why serious scholars neglect consulting NUCMC at their peril.

NUCMC does have limitations, however.

First, it does not dispense travel funds, so it is entirely dependent on the conscience of repositories for reporting. Some report faithfully, some never. The quality and completeness of the descriptions vary widely too.

A second problem is the staggering backlog of cataloging to be done. As the number of repositories reporting collections to us continues to grow, so does our backlog of work. If all reporting ceased tomorrow we would still have several years of work before we cleared our files. Automation may help us catalog more in the future.

A third problem is that NUCMC's descriptions are necessarily brief (perhaps a paragraph long) so they can only hint at the riches contained in a collection. One example might have some bearing on the Hispanic experience in the United States, 1492–1850.

About 120 miles south of Washington, D.C., is the peninsula of Virginia, the long neck of land between the James and York rivers. The region is not (in the public mind, at least) generally associated with the Hispanic experience in the United States. After all, this is the heartland of English Virginia—and the very mention of its name conjures up images of Captain John Smith, Pocahontas, Jamestown, Williamsburg, and Yorktown. Yet many scholars believe that the peninsula was the site of the ill-fated Spanish Jesuit mission to Ajacán, 1570–72.

The one monograph on the topic (*The Spanish Jesuit Mission in Virginia*, by Clifford M. Lewis and Albert Joseph Loomie)[3] drew heavily on the published archives of the Jesuits (Monumenta Historica Societatis Jesu); two large collections of photocopies and transcripts from Spanish archives located at the Library of Congress; as well as three other manuscript collections in the United States: the Buckingham Smith Papers at the New York Historical Society, the John Gilmary Shea Papers at Georgetown University in Washington, and the Charles Campbell Papers at the College of William and Mary in Williamsburg.

All three collections have been listed in NUCMC, but their descriptions were brief. I will quote selectively from the NUCMC cataloging reports.

The Buckingham Smith Papers (MS 60-2926) were described as containing "material on the early history of the Spanish in North America," including transcripts of sixteenth-, seventeenth-, and eighteenth-century papers and books. The John Gilmary Shea Papers (MS 67-95) were described as including transcripts of letters and documents relating to the history of the Catholic church in the United States. And the Charles Campbell Papers (MS 66-269) were listed as including "historical notes" and correspondence with other historians.

None of the descriptions contains an explicit reference to Ajacán or to the Jesuits in the Chesapeake, although we know they contain such material. Such detailed description, unfortunately, is beyond the scope of NUCMC— so I think it underscores the need for a specialized guide to Hispanic manuscripts in the United States that might be able to tackle some of the collections in greater depth than NUCMC can. If the physicists, chemists, foresters, and feminist scholars can produce specialized manuscript guides, why should not the scholars of Hispanic history in the United States? In the meantime, NUCMC will continue producing the familiar blue volumes, and they inevitably will contain more reports of Hispanic collections of interest to you.

In 1988 NUCMC began entering its manuscripts cataloging into the RLIN computer data base. Scholars now have two means of access to NUCMC cataloging: the traditional published volumes and on-line computer access.

The RLIN system, operated by Research Libraries Group (RLG), has a limited membership; only a small percentage of repositories holding manuscript collections in the United States belong to RLG. By reporting to NUCMC, however, non-RLG institutions will have the opportunity of entering their collections into the RLIN data base. This will serve as a conduit by which non-RLG or noncomputerized institutions may enter their manuscript cataloging into an automated system. The access will be a great advance in the creation of a national automated data base for manuscript descriptions. We hope that someday all the old NUCMCs can be entered retrospectively into RLIN, but the way it stands now, only new cataloging will be entered.

Researchers should be aware that participating RLG libraries—about fifty of them—have already begun inputting their own manuscript reports into RLIN directly. OCLC also has a manuscripts data base that should be consulted in any comprehensive search for manuscripts.

I am not quite as sanguine in the belief that automated access to cataloging necessarily will mean improved subject access. A large measure of consistency is lost in subject indexing in great cooperative enterprises with many contributors. That loss of indexing consistency is not always entirely compensated for by computer mechanisms such as context searching and the like.

Despite the problems and challenges that come with automation, however, NUCMC sees the future as a bright one for the on-line description of manuscript collections. It will be able to report more manuscript collections to you more quickly than it has in the past—and the product will be easier for you to use.

Postscript: Progress since 1987

The progress anticipated in the areas of automation and index cumulation in 1988 did indeed come to pass. New NUCMC cataloging began appearing in the automated RLIN data base, and Chadwyck-Healey published (in book form) its *Index to Personal Names in the National Union Catalog of Manuscript Collections, 1959-1984*. In the meantime, two more published volumes of NUCMC have appeared, bringing the total number of collections reported in the printed editions to approximately 60,000.

NOTES

1. Harriet Ostroff, chap. 5 above.
2. *Index to Personal Names in the National Union Catalog of Manuscript Collections, 1959-1984* (Alexandria, VA: Chadyck-Healey, 1988).
3. Clifford M. Lewis and Albert J. Loomie, *The Spanish Jesuit Mission in Virginia, 1570-1572* (Chapel Hill: University of North Carolina Press for Virginia Historical Society, 1953).

PEDRO GONZÁLEZ

7. The Spanish Experience in the United States

Sources of Archives and Reproduction of Documents in Spain

For several reasons the Spanish presence in the territories that today are part of the United States was not as strong as it was in Central and South America. Some disadvantages were the dominant winds that put them outside the regular routes departing from Cádiz, the great distances from Mexico as capital of the viceroyalty, and the dryness of the great plains. Yet it is true that since the early decades of the colonization of the continent, the presence of the first explorers and later of the conquerors and missionaries began to be noticed. It began with Ponce de León's arrival in Florida in 1513 and extended to the greatest expansion, which occurred at the end of the eighteenth century when a great part of the United States—actually the entire South—was linked in some way to the Spanish administration.

The documents that are used for the study of this Spanish presence, and above all, the possibilities of locating them and their reproduction constitute the theme of this chapter. I was asked, as a representative of the State Archives of Spain, to write about the archival sources that exist in Spain and to emphasize the projects and possibilities of the reproduction of the documentation.

Sources of Archives

The current historical archives are the accumulation of the administrative documents that institutions generated in their day. The years purify the documents and give them historical value. And if today we are able to see the documents produced in the past, it is because there existed an institution that generated them during the course of its activity and kept them as archives.

The Spain of the American adventure was a country of long and complex administrative procedures that produced a great quantity of documents in the exercise of its rule. The same bureaucracy of the metropolis was transplanted to the administrative organization overseas. This has enabled us to enjoy today a precious documentary heritage that the years have transformed into a treasure of immeasurable historical value.

The Spanish documents telling the history of America are, in this sense, the papers belonging to the institutions that were involved in the Spanish administration in the Indies. And these institutions, given that America was considered an extension of Castille, were created in imitation of Castillian institutions: the municipality, the audiencia, the viceroyalty, and, as the main institutions, the Consejo de Indias (Council of the Indies) and the Casa de la Contratación (House of Trade).

In addition to the public administration, the Church, bent on its mission to evangelize the New World, left valuable documentary sources.

But where are those papers that reflect the Spanish presence in America preserved? The fundamental depositories are well-known. There is a set of archives in Spain that collected the documentation of the central institutions. Those were mainly the papers of the Council of the Indies and the various secretariats of state that succeeded it, as well as the papers of the House of Trade and related institutions. The archives generated by regional institutions remained for the most part in America. The documents created by the viceroys, the governors, the captains-general, audiencias, and other sources are the core of the National Archives of the Latin American countries. Both the archives of the central authorities in Spain, and those of the regional authorities in America, logically complement each other and both are necessary for a complete study.

Archivo General de Simancas (General Archives of Simancas)

Simancas, the archives that gather in general the documentation of the Spanish House of Austria, accumulated the papers coming from the Council of the Indies, the supreme colonial organization.

When the General Archives of the Indies (AGI) were created in 1785, the bulk of the Simancas American documents were transferred to Seville to become the nucleus of the AGI. However, Simancas still preserves a good number of documents related to the New World, and specifically to the United States, mainly in its sections Secretaría de Estado (Secretariat of State) (which is made up of 8,343 bundles and books classified in 49 series),

Secretaría de Guerra (Secretariat of War) (which is made up of 7,930 bundles and books), and Mapas y Planos (Maps and Plans).

Archivo Histórico Nacional (National Historical Archives)

The largest of the Spanish historical archives is located in Madrid. The National Historical Archives was created in 1866 to collect all documents previously gathered by the Royal Academy of History.

The archives' documentation is not homogeneous or uniform. Rather, it is made up of holdings from the most diverse sources. It can be said that all its sections are discrete archives in themselves with their own personality. The National Historical Archives contain more than 30 km of shelves and more than 160,000 bundles. The building in which they are housed, although constructed expressly for the archives in 1953, is now too small. Consequently, the Ministry of Culture has been planning for some time the construction of a new building.

There are also important documentary sources in the National Historical Archives for the study of the Spanish presence in America. The section of Estado (State), actually a continuation of that of Simancas for the time of the Bourbons (with 8,754 bundles and 1,036 books in addition to 1,071 maps), preserves, among other holdings, the documents from the Spanish Embassy in Washington. The documents of the Council of the Indies are kept in the section of Consejos (Councils), which consist of 53,229 bundles and 3,841 books. Some documents of interest from this council include "Juicios de Residencia" (Trials of Residency), "Ordenes Militares" (Military Orders) and "Clero" (Clergy).

Archivo General de Indias (General Archives of the Indies)

It goes without saying that, despite the importance of the holdings mentioned above, the archives that stand out because of their importance to the Hispanic experience in North America are the General Archives of the Indies.

In 1985, we celebrated the bicentennial of their founding. King Charles III, on the recommendation of his secretary of the Indies, José de Gálvez, ordered their creation. The historian D. Juan Bautista Muñoz, senior cosmographer of the Indies, was charged with the project. The object was to gather in a single place those documents dispersed in Simancas, Cádiz, and Seville, to organize them rationally, and to take advantage of these documents in the writing of a history of Spain in the New World. To house the contents of the archives, the old but magnificent building of the Casa de Lonja of Seville was restored.

The documents kept in the General Archives of the Indies are of exceptional interest to the study and appreciation of the presence of Spain in the Indies. They represent the detailed documentary testimony of Spain's action in the Americas (from the southern United States to Tierra del Fuego) and the Philippines from the end of the fifteenth century to the nineteenth century. In essence, the holdings of the AGI are the papers that emanated from two institutions: the Council of the Indies (and later the secretariats that succeeded the council), with its different governmental and judicial aspects, and second, the House of Trade and similar institutions.

The archives, with their 43,175 bundles, are divided into fifteen sections according to the origin of the holdings. Section V, Gobierno (Government), is itself divided into fifteen subsections. In addition, there is a section of maps and charts organized with documents taken from other sections.

It is interesting to point out the presence of North American investigators in the AGI. During 1986, 842 researchers worked in the AGI. Of this total, 530 were Spaniards; Americans were next with 71.

From the total number of researchers in 1986 distributed by place of origin, we obtain the following percentages:

Spain	62.95%
America	28.62%
Europe (excluding Spain)	7.60%
Asia	0.83%

Researchers from the United States made up 8.43 percent of the total of those engaged in research at the archives. Former years had very similar numbers and percentages.

However, this large number of American researchers in the AGI were not devoted solely to the investigation of North American history. On the contrary, those Americans who investigated the areas related to the history of the United States were in the minority: only 15 of them in 1986. The rest devoted their time to general topics of colonial history or to subjects related to different Latin American countries. By contrast, 17 researchers from different countries declared that they were working on projects concerned with the territories that are now part of the United States.

Holdings of the AGI that are related to the Hispanic presence in North America exist in practically all the sections of the archives. While a major effort has been under way in recent years to inventory the AGI completely, the level of description of these inventories is still not what we would like it to be; it is usually no more than a brief description. A detailed inventory of all the document in the archives will be a job of many years.

The AGI is currently the object of an ambitious computerization project that will include the digitizing and storage on optical disk of a large number of documents, a subject discussed below in more detail.

Other Archives

A presence as lasting as that of Spain in America would logically be reflected in many documental holdings. Until now, we have considered only those archives that contain documentation from the Central Administration. But there are numerous other archives where it is possible to find other kinds of information; including religious, military, judicial, notarial, and municipal.

The General Directorate of Archives and Libraries, under the auspices of UNESCO, published a *Guide of Sources for the History of Spanish America* in 1966 in two volumes. More than 150 centers with documentation related to this topic are described. Contained in many of them are papers with information related to the Spanish presence in the United States. Briefly, let us recall some of them.

The Archives of the Royal Chancelleries of Valladolid and Granada, in their series of Pleitos (Litigations), contain information about people who resided in America but who had disputes on property and rights in Spain.

The Archives of the Ministry of Foreign Affairs preserve nineteenth-century documents from embassies and consulates, some of the latter having been located in United States territory.

In the Ministry of Justice are preserved files for the granting of titles of nobility. Some of the records refer to persons with central roles in the Spanish presence in the United States, such as Bernardo de Gálvez, who in 1783 was granted the title of count of Gálvez.

In the Archives of the National Patrimony, which contain holdings from the Royal House, there is a series called Estampilla Real (Royal Stamp), made up of the records of all appointments that required the royal signature. This series starts in 1759 and ends in 1931. It contains appointments of viceroys, governors, archbishops, bishops, and others.

It is possible to find scores of facts about people who lived or worked in America in the archives of the municipalities, of the parishes, and of the public scribes. However, finding this information requires long and detailed work.

The Archives of the General Headquarters of the Armada contain a series, Corso y Presas (Patent of Piracy and Booty) (1784–1837), and another called Expediciones a Indias (Expeditions to the Indies), which is of great interest for the study of the independence epoch.

The Naval Museum holds documentation related to my topic in the Navarrete Collection, in the collection Mapas y Planos, and in the series Manuscritos; they are all related to naval topics.

There are also many private archives, such as the archives of the dukes of Alba, of the Infantado, and of the counts of Revillagigedo.

Some libraries, such as the National Library of Madrid, contain important manuscript collections. In the National Library there is a Manuscritos section (of which there is a catalog listing the manuscripts that refer to America by Julián Paz, 1933; in addition, there is the catalog of Manuscritos de América en las Bibliotecas de España (Manuscripts of America in the Libraries of Spain) by J. Tudela de la Orden, 1954), the Incunables y Raros section (Incunabula and Rarities), and Hispanoamérica, although the last two sections also include bibliographic holdings. An excellent cartographic collection containing a good series of maps of America is also in the National Library.

The holdings of the Royal Academy of History are important; to these archives belong, among others, the Muñoz Collection, with its 76 volumes of originals and copies prepared by the founder of the General Archives of the Indies; the Boturini Collection; and the Jesuit Collection, which contains a part (the primary one) of the documents of the company that had such a great impact on the history of America.

The University Archives of Seville preserve the holdings of the old University of Mareantes, founded in Seville in the sixteenth century. Also of great importance are the Archivos de Protocolos (Notarial Archives) of Seville and Cádiz, where vast quantities of documents related to the varied business in the Indies have been preserved through the institution of the notary public. However, to search in them, one must work document by document. Currently, there is a project to move the Archivo de Protocolos of Seville—in order to provide suitable accommodations for it—to the new building constructed for the Historical Provincial Archives.

The religious archives must also be considered. Besides the already mentioned parish archives are those of the bishops and cathedrals. Of more interest are the archives of the religious orders that participated in the evangelization of the Indies. For example, the important Jesuit archives are kept in different places, mainly in the aforementioned National Historical Archives and the Royal Academy of History, as well as in the Archives of the Toledan Province of the Company of Jesus in Alcalá de Henares.

Reproduction of Documents of Interest for the History of the Spanish Presence in the United States

The enormous quantity of documents extant in the different archives has been affected to some extent by the political and administrative changes that have come about in Spain in recent years, changes I would like to mention, albeit briefly.

The evolution of the former regime into a constitutional democracy constitutes the fundamental change. Article 105b of the Spanish Constitution of 1978 formally recognizes access to information as a constitutional right, with logical exceptions: "The law shall regulate . . . citizens' access to the archives and administrative records, except where the security and defense of the State, the investigation of crimes, and personal privacy are affected." The first legal development of this article is Law 16/1985 of June 25, for the Spanish Historical Patrimony, which is followed by diverse regulations, among them one about the archives.

At the same time, the constitution establishes the judicial bases by which Spain has passed from a rigidly centralized administration to a decentralized one that is divided into seventeen autonomous communities. This new form of the state has developed through the promulgation and application of the Statutes of Autonomy, and, in matters related to the archives, by the transfer of authority and services.

The development of these principles has led to the transfer by the state to the autonomous communities of an important part of its former authority and has even led to a new archival map. The archives that continue to depend directly on the state are only those of a national character. The administration of those of a regional or provincial nature has been transferred to the autonomous communities, although the state maintains its "title of ownership." Because of this, currently only the National Historical Archives, the General Archives of Simancas, the General Archives of the Indies, the Archives of the Crown of Aragon, and the Archives of the Chancellery of Valladolid remain dependent upon the Ministry of Culture; the rest of the regional or provincial archives have been or are about to be transferred.

Logically, the administrative archives continue to depend on the administration that created them, just as the private archives (such as the ecclesiastical and those belonging to individuals) depend on their titular owners, although always subject to general legislation. The state, however, is required to make a census of the assets that comprise the documental patrimony and must see that these assets are adequately preserved and protected, no matter who their titular owner may be. In the same fashion, all the titular holders of the assets that make up the Spanish documental patrimony are obligated "to allow researchers, who shall make a request beforehand, to study them. Individuals may be exempt from carrying out this last obligation, in the case where it would occasion an infringement of the right to personal and family privacy, and to their own image, in the terms established by the regulatory legislation on this matter."

Microfilming

The law, in summary, has clearly recognized the right of citizens to access the archives. But it is also greatly concerned with the better preservation of the holdings, and to slow or stop the progressive deterioration to which they are subject because of their continual use and handling. Better dissemination and accessibility of the documents, and at the same time their better preservation, are achieved largely through mass reproduction, which avoids repeated reproduction of the same documents. Through the use of microfilming methods, and, from now on, digitizing systems, it is possible to repeat the copying process as many times as needed without having to return to the original.

The Spanish State Archives have responded by establishing laboratories in different archives and by creating the National Microfilm Center. The reproduction of documents in the Spanish Archives are governed by two different initiatives: first, the microfilming of documents made by specific petition from a researcher, normally carried out in the archives' own laboratories; and second, the reproduction of series from different archives as a security measure to complement other series, and to copy microfilm editions that have been made by the National Microfilm Center under the Ministry of Culture.

At present, the microfilm center offers for sale the following editions related to our topic:

From the AGI:

1. From the section of Cuba: Documents of western Florida and Louisiana, 556 rolls of film, which comprise 332,206 frames (Publication numbers 78, 87, 105, and 106).

2. From Escribanía de la Cámara (Notary of the Chamber), in addition to 57 rolls containing 35,101 frames that correspond to residencies of several viceroys, there is a publication including "Pleitos de Florida (1577–1754)" ("Litigations of Florida") in 4 rolls containing 2,223 frames (Publication 103).

3. From the section of Gobierno, Audiencia of Santo Domingo, there are 20 rolls containing 13,311 frames, including letters from governors of Florida (1566–1765) (Publication 104). From the Audiencia of Mexico there are 104 rolls and from Indiferente General (Miscellaneous), 67.

4. From the section of Justicia, in addition to two rolls containing the inventories, there are the following publications: from the Audiencia of Guadalajara, 19 rolls including 10,223 frames (Publications 6 and 86). From the Audiencia of Mexico there are 67 rolls, with 50,184 frames (Publication numbers 76 and 108). From the Audiencia of Santo Domingo there are 85 rolls, with 52,732 frames, in Publication 82.

5. From the section of Mapas y Planos there is in one roll, or in microfiche, the series of Mapas y Planos de Florida y Luisiana, including 459 frames (Publication 89).

6. From the Section of Patronato (Patronage), there is its inventory (2 rolls, 870 frames, Publication 2) and Bulas y Breves (Bulls and Briefs) (4 rolls, 1,171 frames, Publication 33).

7. From the section of Contratación, in addition to its inventory (9 rolls, 2,700 frames, Publication 4), we have 11 rolls of Passengers to the Indies, including 6,898 frames (Publication 79).

From the General Archives of Simancas:

1. From the section Secretaría de Guerra—América there is a set of publications that contain the "Hojas de Servicios Militares en América" (Papers of Military Services in America), from which Publications 19 and 20 correspond to New Spain, with 12 rolls and 6,136 frames, and Publication 11 corresponds to Santo Domingo, one roll with 500 frames.

2. From the Dirección General del Tesoro (General Directorate of the Treasury) there was published the inventory of "Títulos de Indias" (Titles of the Indies), 76 rolls, with 48,731 frames.

From the National Historical Archives:

1. From the section of Códices, the Cedulario (File of Decrees) de Indias (Publication 35, with 24 rolls, 16,155 frames) and the Dictionary of Government and Legislation of the Indies (Publication 36, with 6 rolls and 4,588 frames).

2. From the section of Consejos, the Collection of Decrees and Royal Orders of the Indies (Publication 94, with 6 rolls and 3,205 frames).

3. And in the section of Estado there are 4 publications (numbers 16, 67, 88, and 99) concerning diplomatic relations between Spain and the United States in 98 rolls and 64,510 frames.

The resources available to the microfilm center have not been as adequate as would have been desired. For this reason we have accepted, for certain programs, the cooperation of foreign organizations interested in specific series from some archives. Agreements have been reached with several institutions, such as with the University of Florida in 1981, to microfilm 113 bundles related to Florida. These bundles were taken from the section of Papeles de la Capitanía General de Cuba in the General Archives of the Indies. The university agreed to pay for the ordering of the documents as well as for the microfilming, which would be made by the microfilm center. Similarly, the university agreed to consider these reproductions scientifically valuable and a tool for research and reference only and not for commercial purposes. Florida agreed not to issue copies of microfilms without permission from the General Directorate of Fine Arts and Archives.

Another agreement of this type has been signed by the Ministry of Culture with the Genealogical Society of Utah (1984), which is interested in the reproduction of holdings from other Spanish archives. In this case, the desired documents, from the Provincial Historical Archives, included Notarial Protocols, Population Census, Hidalguías (Knighthoods), Emigration Records, and Military Files. This agreement is different from the one with Florida, since the society does the microfilming directly using its own personnel and materials, working under the archives' labor regulations, and abiding by the quality standards of the National Microfilm Center. The center retains the negatives for security reasons and for further reproductions. The Genealogical Society keeps a second set of negatives for the reproduction of copies for its own centers, but it may not issue any copies for other institutions or persons unless it is authorized explicitly by the microfilm center.

Currently, the National Microfilm Center, which has undergone several phases of administrative reorganization, is acquiring new momentum, and its potential will be augmented by an increase in its staff and equipment.

But, besides the now classic microfilm system, the Spanish Ministry of Culture is also interested in the possibilities offered by new technology in the area of reproduction and dissemination of documents.

Project to Computerize the General Archives of the Indies

The most important project for the reproduction of documents being supported by the Ministry of Culture is the one to computerize the General Archives of the Indies.

In the framework of the activities commemorating the Quincentennial of the discovery of America, the Ministry of Culture, IBM España, and the Ramón Areces Foundation signed an agreement of cooperation in 1986 for the design and development of an automated information system for the General Archives of the Indies. The project will extend to the end of 1992 with a budget of approximately 1 billion pesetas, around $8 million.

The project includes the design and development of an integrated computer system for the AGI with three basic sections: a data base with textual information that will gather information now dispersed in inventories, catalogs, and indexes; a user transaction system for the accreditation of researchers, access control and in situ work, requests for the movement of holdings, usage statistics, as well as other purposes; and the digitizing of documents, their storage in optical disks, and their display on high-resolution screens.

The AGI currently contains 43,175 bundles. If we estimate around 1,000 sheets per bundle, mostly written on both sides, we guess there are approximately 80 million pages in the archive. The computerization project plans to digitize 11 percent of the documents in the archive, or more than 4,000 bundles containing approximately 9 million pages, before the end of 1992.

Which documents will be digitized? Several criteria were considered. Statistical studies were made on the series that have been most frequently used during the last few years. The state of description of the series was considered, as well as the state of their preservation. An attempt was made to cover as much as possible the geographical spectrum to which the documents referred, and the significance of the documents in the light of the Quincentennial was also considered.

The result of these studies is a list of series from the following sections:

Section	Subsection	Number of Bundles
1. Patronato		305
2. Contratación		531
3. Gobierno		
	Audiencia of Guatemala	203
	Audiencia of Guadalajara	78
	Audiencia of Caracas	3
	Audiencia of Santo Domingo	300
	Audiencia of Panama	121
	Audiencia of Quito	110
	Audiencia of Santa Fe	290
	Audiencia of Lima	380
	Audiencia of Chile	72
	Audiencia of Charcas	158
	Audiencia of Buenos Aires	6
	Audiencia of the Philippines	111
	Audiencia of Mexico	430
	Indiferente General	889
9. Estado		105
	Total	4,092

Once the documents to be digitized were selected, another statistical study was made on the use of these series during the last few years. The number of requests from 1984 to 1985 that had as their object dossiers of the selected series was fed to a computer. The relation between the number of dossiers and the number of references was established.

The results are excellent. According to these facts, very high benefits would have been obtained from digitizing this 10 percent of the archive: approximately 30 percent of the requests for documents from the archives during the time period considered could have been met directly on screen.

Later, in 1990, the statistical studies on the performance of the series selected were repeated using data obtained from the user management program that was already operating. The results are encouraging. If we manage to meet our goal of 10 percent, we will be able to deal with over 30 percent of the reading applications made on the holdings from the search room.

From the conference celebration until the publication of the proceedings, the development of the project has continued. At this moment we have installed in Seville the prototype of the system, with a subset of the final functions in order to receive the users' feedback.

Today, we have thirty people to do the scanning job, working with 15 scanners in two shifts. About 1.5 million document pages have been recorded on optical disk. And recently, in May 1990, we decided to initiate an important change in the strategy of digitization. Because there are document series in other Spanish archives dealing with the colonization of America, we shall scan them also. In Seville we are in the process of digitizing 525 bundles of the Secretaria de Guerra (War Secretariat) from the Archivo General de Simancas (AGS). The objective is clear: the AGI will have a complete copy of the Indies records that it does not hold within its own walls. The AGS will also benefit from the project once the entire system network has been installed that is planned for this and the other national historical archives.

Currently, technology is solving some of our problems, but it cannot yet solve all of them. And the process of digitizing must be complemented with other tasks, which continue to demand an enormous effort from our personnel: mainly, the increase in the work of describing the documents. After a long period of work, the AGI is now completely inventoried. However, the level of description of the different finding aids is unfortunately very superficial and generally offers only a few lines of information for many pages of documentation.

The Ministry of Culture is aware of this problem, which poses a great challenge for the Project to Computerize the General Archives of the Indies. Only with a deeper and more complex description in the textual data base will the direct consultation of documents on screen be made useful and feasible. Because of this, plans have been made to extend and deepen the description of those series of documents that have been selected for digitizing. The overall project currently under way will last until the end of 1992 and will be ultimately useful only with a deeper and more detailed index and level of description to the finding aids.

Conclusion

The Ministry of Culture, through the Directorate of the State Archives, is open to anything that entails a better understanding and dissemination of our history. Our human, economic, and technical resources are not always what we would like to have. However, challenged by the celebration of the Quincentennial of the Discovery of America, Spain is making a very special effort in the area of archives, specifically in the reproduction of documents about the Spanish presence and actions in America.

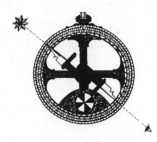

2 · Research

Introduction to Part 2

Charles Hudson came to the Hispanic experience in North America with the perspective of an anthropologist. His interest in Spanish documentation of the sixteenth century is specific and urgent as he and his students attempt to recreate the culture of American native peoples at the time of the conquest and in the centuries immediately following. Whereas a number of chapters in this book deal with general themes and call for general goals, Hudson tells us the exciting story of how anthropologists are often dependent on the meaning of a single Spanish word or phrase in their painstaking work of deciphering early American history.

John Kessell takes a lighter stroke to his work as he brings us the view of the historian of the Southwest. He describes the brave new world of the computerized historian and finds something lacking. He gently chides the man before the monitor but provides us—like Lyon—with the thrill of searching down documents and collections dealing with a man central to the history of early New Mexico.

CHARLES HUDSON

8. Research on the Eastern Spanish Borderlands

My purpose here will not be to comprehensively survey research on the eastern Spanish borderlands but rather to discuss recent research on what is the most crucial problem in the early history of the southern United States.[1] It is a problem that in truth is made up of three separate but related problems: What was the nature of native societies in the sixteenth-century Southeast? What were the locations and domains of these societies? How were these societies transformed into the very different native societies that Europeans encountered in the interior of the Southeast in the late seventeenth and early eighteenth centuries? If these questions can be answered, it will be possible to add over a century to southern history.[2]

These have always been crucial problems in the early history of the South. In the nineteenth century, for example, it seemed obvious that the huge earthen mounds and ornate Indian artifacts discovered in the Southeast had not been made by the Indians who lived in the South in the nineteenth century. They were too few, too dispirited, and given to drink. Given the prevailing racist ideology and romantic idiom of the time, the most popular theory to explain the existence of the ancient earthworks and artifacts was that they had been made by a different and superior race of people—Moundbuilders—who had occupied the land prior to the coming of the Indians. The identity and place of origin of this race of Moundbuilders varied from one theorist to another. To some it seemed that the mounds had been built by Israelites; to others Carthaginians, or the army of Alexander the Great, or Welshmen, or Basques—the list goes on and on.[3] The common theme in these theories is that it made sense to nineteenth-century thinkers to explain the unknown and mysterious in terms of the known and familiar. The only real innovation in this line of thought was devised quite recently by Erich von Daniken, who explained the unknown and mysterious in terms of the unknown and mysterious. According to von Daniken, the Moundbuilders (of South America and presumably North America) came from other planets.[4]

But alongside these devotees of the racist, the romantic, and the downright fantastic, there were always cooler heads. Thomas Jefferson excavated a mound on his estate in Virginia, and after examining the contents of the mound he concluded that it could have been built by Indians. He saw no reason for a more far-fetched explanation.[5] An even stronger argument in favor of Indians as the builders of the mounds was made in 1873 by Charles Colcock Jones, Jr., in his *Antiquities of the Southern Indians.*[6] Jones had read a translation of a firsthand chronicle of the Hernando de Soto expedition in which it could be seen that De Soto and his men had encountered large and powerful Indian societies. The chronicler specifically described mounds that the Indians had built and used as substructures for temples and the houses of important men. Jones's interpretation was confirmed in 1891, when the monumental report on mound exploration by the Bureau of American Ethnology was published.[7] For most serious scholars, this laid the Moundbuilder theory to rest.

But granted that the mounds were built by Indians encountered by De Soto and other sixteenth-century explorers, what sort of people were they, and where, exactly, did they live? As far as I have been able to determine, none of the sixteenth-century Spaniards who explored the South was very much interested in matters that we would today call ethnographic or sociological. In contrast, quite a number of early French and English observers were interested in such matters. This is clear as early as the sixteenth century in the writings of the French Huguenots who attempted to found a colony at the mouth of the St. Johns River in Florida.[8] The impulse is even more evident among French and English observers in the late seventeenth century and throughout the eighteenth century.[9] The reason for the difference seems to be that because of the Protestant Reformation and the Enlightenment, the French and the English were more receptive to the fact that people could differ fundamentally in how they thought and lived. The mere fact of being culturally different did not indicate heresy or Satanism.

But it remains that the only firsthand observers of the Indians of the interior of the sixteenth-century Southeast were Spaniards who were little interested in human differences for their own sake. Bits and pieces of ethnographic and sociological observation are contained in the documents of the sixteenth-century Spanish explorers, and they must be squeezed for all the information they contain.

Most of our present understanding of the cultures and societies of native people of the sixteenth-century Southeast has been unearthed by archaeologists in research conducted during the past fifty years, and a great portion of this has been done in the past fifteen years. Archaeologists have evidence that the Mississippian culture or life-way emerged in the Southeast about A.D. 1000, lasted until the time of Spanish exploration, and then it declined.

Mississippian societies were not bands or tribes, but chiefdoms. Hierarchy and social inequality did exist in these societies, but their populations numbered in the thousands rather than in the millions, and they did not approach the complexity and sophistication of the state-level societies of Mexico and South America. The economic basis of these Mississippian chiefdoms was the cultivation of corn, beans, and squash on naturally rich but scarce soils, with a supplement of wild foods that they got by hunting, fishing, and collecting. They were farmers in an important way, but they were also hunters, fishermen, and collectors. Consistent with their ranked social structure, Mississippian societies had communities of different sizes, ranging from large political and ceremonial centers (almost always at mound sites), secondary centers (often at mound sites), and small villages to even in some places tiny homesteads comprised of one or more families. Warfare was waged between some chiefdoms, and in places it was waged at a high level, as evidenced by the fact that towns were surrounded by palisades constructed of large wooden posts.[10]

Archaeologists specialize in "reading" the material products and by-products of societies in the past. They have been able to reconstruct quite a bit about the material and economic life of Mississippian people. They have reconstructed at least some features of Mississippian social structure, but they can tell us relatively little about Mississippian polities, that is, societies to which people belonged or with which they were politically aligned. Membership in a polity need not be directly reflected in material culture. Beyond this, archaeologists can tell us very little to nothing at all about aspects of Mississippian culture that were largely or completely based on shared understandings. By this I refer to such matters as belief systems and languages. Hence, when archaeologists discuss the communities and societies they attempt to reconstruct, they refer to them as "phases" and give them arbitrary names. For instance, they refer to sites on the Coosawattee River in Georgia dating to the early sixteenth century as belonging to Barnett phase; to those of the same time on the Little Tennessee and lower French Broad rivers as Dallas phase, and so on. Thus, when one moves from historic time back into prehistoric time, one moves from familiar named societies to distributions of material artifacts bearing arbitrarily chosen names.

Archaeologists have not been notably successful in figuring out who lived where in the sixteenth-century Southeast. This crucial first step has been easier to achieve in the western borderlands than in the eastern borderlands. Compare, for example, John Francis Bannon's map of southwestern towns and pueblos with his map of southeastern tribes.[11] The former is admirably detailed, whereas the latter is detailed only in locating sixteenth-and seventeenth-century Spanish missions and a few Indian groups who lived along the coast. This interior is largely blank.

The reason for this difference between the Southwest and the Southeast is that for Indian horticulturalists, the Southeast was a better place to live. The Southeast is laced with rivers and creeks, and along many of these streams there are deposits of rich alluvial soil that were ideal for Indian agriculture. In the Southwest there are not that many places where corn could be cultivated. Consequently, when historians and anthropologists began tracing the routes of sixteenth-century explorers on modern maps, the places they could have visited were few in number in the Southwest and many in the Southeast. Anyone who doubts this should look at the map prepared by the U.S. De Soto Commission, which shows De Soto's route as reconstructed by all the major scholars who had attempted it.[12] I have referred to this as the spaghetti map because one would get much the same effect if one took a handful of spaghetti and threw it against a map of the Southeast.

In 1980 I began collaborating with Marvin Smith and Chester DePratter in an attempt to figure out where the De Soto expedition went. We quickly found that when we used the De Soto narratives alone, it was possible to take the expedition almost anywhere. Start where you will in most parts of the Southeast, and you find that in all directions there are streams, arable lands, and very frequently Indian archaeological sites. At first we made no more progress than previous scholars had.

A way out of this impasse came when we began reading an account of Juan Pardo's second expedition, which was written by his scribe and notary, Juan de la Bandera. This document had been translated by Herbert Ketcham and had lain for many years in the North Carolina state archives, where it was little used.[13] Pardo was sent from Santa Elena, near Beaufort, South Carolina, into the interior in 1566 and again in 1567 by Pedro Menéndez de Avilés. Menéndez ordered Pardo to pacify the Indians, find a road to the silver mines in Zacatecas, and to return to Santa Elena by the following spring so that he could be on hand in case the French attacked. Pardo's impossible mission was abandoned when, well into his second journey, he was confronted by a very large force of Indians who threatened to attack him. Prudently, he returned to Santa Elena. Imprudently, he left most of his men behind defending a string of five small forts. The Indians soon overran these forts, and very few of his men were ever seen again.

As we read the Bandera document, it was clear that Pardo had visited five of the same towns De Soto had visited a quarter of a century earlier. He encountered these towns in the same order in which De Soto had encountered them, and they were described as being in the same kind of terrain. Moreover, the Bandera document was far more detailed than any of the De Soto documents for this segment of the route. Using this greatly detailed itinerary, we tried every possible route leading from Santa Elena northward to the Appalachian Mountains. The best fit was achieved by taking Pardo north from Santa Elena and then east to the Wateree-Catawba River and along that river to its headwaters in the Blue Ridge Mountains, and from there through Swannanoa Gap to the French Broad River, and then along its banks to the Tennessee Valley.[14]

With Pardo's route plotted on a map, we returned to De Soto's route armed with independently established locations for the Indian towns of Hymahi (Guiomae), Cofitachequi, Ylapi, Xuala (Joara), and Chiaha (see map 1). We began with De Soto departing from his 1539–40 winter campsite at Apalachee. Scholars have known for many years that Apalachee was located in the vicinity of Tallahassee, Florida, and recent archaeological discoveries now indicate that some, if not all, of De Soto's men camped within the city limits of Tallahassee.[15] We were thus able to start De Soto at Tallahassee, and using a rate of speed of no more than about seventeen miles per day, geographical features mentioned in the documents, and known archaeological sites along the way, we were able to reconstruct his route through Georgia and into Pardo country, all the way to Chiaha, on Zimmerman's Island near present Dandridge, Tennessee.[16]

With this segment of the De Soto route in hand, we gained insight into the modus operandi of the expedition. De Soto and party moved at about the same rate of speed Pardo did, and they were guided by Indians who almost always followed clear trails. While DeSoto and his men wished to find precious substances, they had to find food. They sought out the central towns of the most populous Indian societies because that is where the food either was stored or could most conveniently be extracted or extorted from the people.

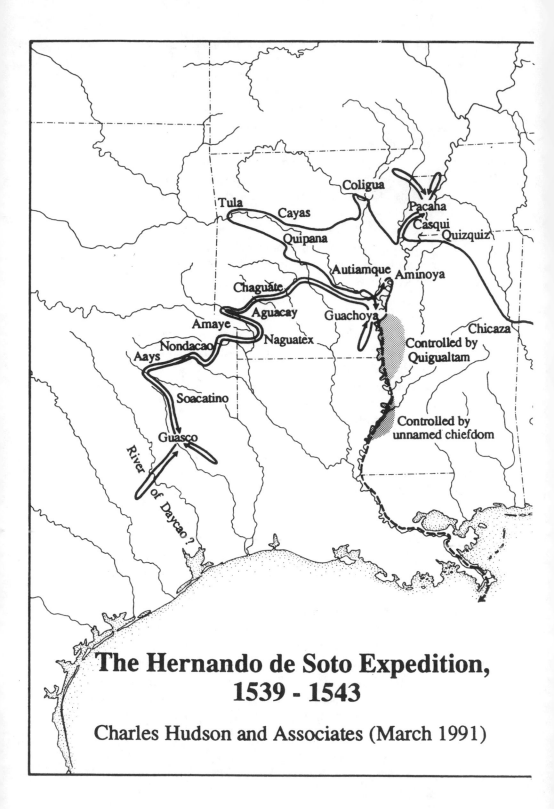

The Hernando de Soto Expedition, 1539 - 1543

Charles Hudson and Associates (March 1991)

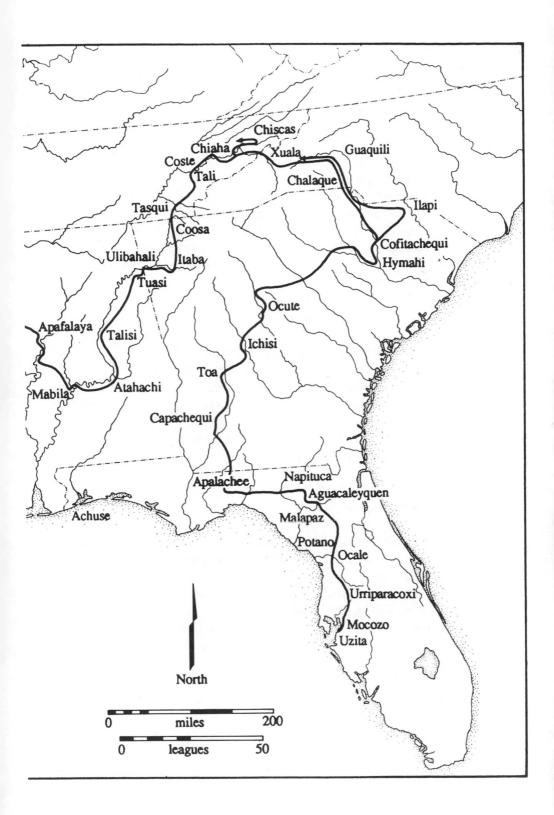

Chiscas

Chiaha

Coste

Tali

Xuala

Guaquili

Chalaque

Tasqui

Coosa

Ilapi

Ulibahali

Itaba

Cofitachequi

Hymahi

Tuasi

Ocute

Apafalaya

Talisi

Ichisi

Mabila

Atahachi

Toa

Capachequi

Apalachee

Napituca

Achuse

Aguacaleyquen

Malapaz

Potano

Ocale

Urriparacoxi

Mocozo

Uzita

North

0   miles   200

0   leagues   50

From Chiaha we continued on, tracing their route southwest down the Ridge and Valley province through the northwestern corner of Georgia, and from there down a trail that lay to the east of the Coosa River to Athahachi, a town of Chief Tascaluza near present Montgomery, Alabama, and from there to Mabila, in the vicinity of the lower Cahaba River, west of present Selma.[17] At Mabila, on October 18, 1540, De Soto and his men fought a desperate battle against a large force of Indians.

We have published our reconstruction of these two segments of De Soto's route, and our research on remaining segments of the route is in various stages of completion.[18] One immediate benefit of our reconstruction of De Soto's route from Chiaha to Mabila is that it has provided town locations that enabled us to make sense out of the movements and activities of Tristán de Luna's men in the interior in 1559–61.[19]

We are more confident in the accuracy of some parts of our De Soto route than we are of others, but we expect that every part of the route will be challenged, and debate is likely to continue for quite some time.[20] Parts of our route can be tested through archaeological research, although such testing is by no means as unambiguous as one would wish it to be.

The routes of exploration followed by De Soto, Luna, and Pardo are interesting in themselves, but their real importance is that they are primary evidence in shedding light on the problem discussed at the beginning of this chapter. From the Bandera document, for example, it is clear that there were three distinct levels of authority in sixteenth-century southeastern societies. The *orata* appears to have been the headman of a village or a small political unit. The *mico* was a chief who could have many villages under his or her authority. But above all of these was a paramount chief whose Indian title, if indeed there was one, was not recorded by the Spaniards. The territories under the control or influence of some of these paramount chiefs were far larger than we expected them to be, and they were more culturally and linguistically heterogeneous than we expected.[21]

In going from Apalachee to Mabila, De Soto encountered four paramount chiefdoms: Ocute, Cofitachequi, Coosa, and Tascaluza. Because of problems in archaeological information in the area of Tascaluza, it is not possible at present to delimit the domain of this polity. But evidence on the other three is easier to interpret. The paramount chiefdom of Ocute had its center of population along the Oconee River. The principal town of the chiefdom appears to have been at the Shoulderbone archaeological site north of present Sparta, Georgia. The domain of Ocute extended up the Oconee River at least to the Scull Shoals site near Greensboro, and perhaps beyond, and it extended downstream to fifteen or twenty miles south of Milledge-ville, and perhaps farther. Beyond this, it is possible—though it cannot be proved—that the power or influence of Ocute extended to the Guale coast and to the chiefdom of Ichisi on the Ocmulgee River, centered near present Macon.[22]

When De Soto reached Ocute, he learned that this chiefdom was at war with the chiefdom of Cofitachequi. One chief told him that they had ever been at war with Cofitachequi and that they constantly went about under arms. When De Soto set out from Ocute to go to Cofitachequi he was surprised when he found that he had to cross an uninhabited wilderness over a hundred miles wide. This uninhabited zone stretched all the way from the drainage of the Oconee River in Georgia to the drainage of the Catawba-Wateree River in South Carolina. The Savannah River, which lay in the middle of this wilderness, was uninhabited for almost its entire length. A century or so prior to the De Soto expedition, Indians were numerous in several towns along the Savannah River. But for reasons that are not yet fully understood, they abandoned their towns and moved away.[23] In several other places on his expedition De Soto found wildernesses between warring chief-doms, but none so vast as the wilderness of Ocute.

It was not so long ago that many historians assumed that most of North America was a vast wilderness unmodified by man. And now we learn that in the sixteenth century wildernesses did indeed exist, but at least some of them were caused or at least shaped by social or political factors. That is, there were areas that might be wilderness in one century but inhabited in the next century, and vice versa.

The paramount chiefdom of Cofitachequi had its center near present Camden, South Carolina. The population center of this chiefdom stretched northward to about present Charlotte and southward to about the junction of the Congaree and Wateree rivers. But the influence of the paramount chief of Cofitachequi stretched northward to the edge of the Blue Ridge Mountains, eastward to the middle course of the Pee Dee River, and south-ward perhaps to the Atlantic coast.[24]

The principal language of Cofitachequi belonged to the Eastern Musko-gean language family. But some of the towns that were subject to Cofita-chequi spoke Catawban languages, and some of them may have spoken Iro-quoian languages. Yuchian is another language that may have been spoken in this area, and it is possible that languages of completely unknown language families may have been present.[25]

When De Soto crossed the mountains and reached the Tennessee Valley, he entered the territory of the paramount chiefdom of Coosa. The central town of this chiefdom was at the Little Egypt archaeological site near Carters, Georgia. The center of population of Coosa lay on a ten-mile stretch of the Coosawattee River. The power and influence of Coosa extended northeast to the vicinity of about Newport, Tennessee, northwest to present Chattanooga, and southward to about Sylacauga, Alabama. It is probable that the Appalachian Mountains served as a wilderness between Cofitachequi and Coosa, though small populations of people did live in that area.

The principal language of Coosa also belonged to the Eastern Muskogean language family. But some members of Coosa spoke the Koasati language (a separate subfamily of Muskogean), and still other languages may have been spoken by the people of Coosa.[26] There is archaeological evidence of cultural differences among the people of the paramount chiefdom of Coosa, just as there were among the people of Cofitachequi.[27]

The research I have just reviewed is making it possible to draw a map of the social geography of the sixteenth-century Southeast comparable in fullness and accuracy to existing maps of the sixteenth-century Southwest. It is a map whose surface is adorned by large paramount chiefdoms, some of which were at war with each other and separated by uninhabited buffer zones. Many of these chiefdoms bear names that disappeared during the next century or so. The social and political texture of the sixteenth century was far different from what it was in the early eighteenth century, when the native populations were much smaller, less hierarchically organized, and known by such names as Upper Creeks, Lower Creeks, Catawbas, Cherokees, Chickasaws, and Choctaws.

Elsewhere I have termed the period from 1568 to about 1670 the great black hole of southern history.[28] There was no significant European penetration into the interior of the Southeast during this time, and yet this is when momentous changes were occurring—a period when a numerous people, living for over 10,000 years in splendid isolation from people in the Old World, had to face the consequences of being reunited with them. A significant advance in our understanding of this period has been achieved by Marvin Smith in his recently published *Archaeology of Aboriginal Culture Change in the Interior Southeast*.[29] Smith has been able to identify a number of European artifacts found at various archaeological sites in the Southeast that were manufactured during fairly short periods of time. Most of these were artifacts that Europeans traded or gave to the Indians. Using artifacts such as glass beads, iron tools, and brass ornaments and bells, Smith has been able to establish a chronology for the interior Southeast that divides the period from 1525 to 1670 into four intervals of thirty to forty years each. Though it may seem strange to historians, the ability to date a protohistoric archaeological site to within thirty to forty years is no mean achievement.

When Smith examined the archaeological data for the areas where the chiefdoms of Coosa and Ocute were located, he found evidence of a sharp demographic decline, social collapse, migration, and the coalescence of the survivors of once disparate communities into new societies. The cause of the falling population, as has long been known, was Old World bacteria and viruses. But Smith has evidence that in some places these diseases began taking their toll very soon after the sixteenth-century Spanish explorations, and this declining population had an impact on the chiefdoms very quickly. Archaeological sites become smaller in size and fewer in number. The people ceased building mounds by 1600. By 1700 many of the survivors of the paramount chiefdom of Ocute coalesced to form one rather small town—Oconee Old Town—little more than a way station on one of the English trading paths.

The fate of the paramount chiefdom of Coosa was similar to that of Ocute. The only real difference was that the people of Coosa were able to coalesce in the area along the lower Coosa and Tallapoosa rivers, at a farther remove from the English colonies than was possible for the people of Ocute. Here they became known as Creeks in the early eighteenth century. Their coalescence apparently began around 1670 or 1680, and the evidence is that the people of Coosa were fleeing from other Indians who had been armed with guns.

To this I can add that the decline of Cofitachequi was similar to that of Ocute. By 1700, when John Lawson traveled from Charlestown to the backcountry of the Carolinas, the grand chiefdom of Cofitachequi had ceased to exist. Its name had disappeared from the map. In its place were several small remnant populations of societies that had once been tributary to Cofitachequi. And it is clear from Lawson that these people were vying for favor from the English traders.

It is to be hoped that archaeologists and historians will replicate Smith's study in other parts of the interior South. It is likely that they will find that much the same course of events occurred almost everywhere. This was as follows: Before European penetration the land was divided up among a series of three-level paramount chiefdoms, sometimes with uninhabited wildernesses between them. After about 1540, Old World diseases took a swift and terrible toll of life, so that the paramount chiefdoms could no longer operate as before. These large polities broke up into smaller units with only one or two levels of command. Then, around 1670—though sooner in some places—the southern Indians began to be incorporated into the modern world economy as hunters and slave catchers, and at that time they began to coalesce to form new kinds of societies.

I would like to append the following hypothesis to Smith's interpretation: The dislocation of native societies in the Southeast was greatest where there was closest contact with English traders. It was the germs and viruses that caused the native population to plummet, but it was the Indians armed with English guns, and most particularly the slave catchers, who caused them to pick up and relocate their towns many miles away. A very simple test of this hypothesis could be had by comparing the geographical stability of Indian societies in seventeenth-century Spanish Florida to those in the Carolinas, Tennessee, and Alabama.[30]

A history of the Southeast from 1540 to 1670 will soon be within our grasp. Its progress will depend upon archaeological research that will test and amplify this new conception of protohistoric social geography and of the social transformations that occurred in this period. But it will also depend upon historians who have the skills to do research in Spanish documents. Almost any snippet of information on Indians in the interior of the Southeast could be important. Even a recorded word or two of native languages can be crucial. For example, two place-names on the Little Tennessee River mentioned in the Pardo documents argue strongly that the sixteenth-century inhabitants of this river spoke a Muskogean language. Archaeologists have debated for several decades about whether the Cherokees were long-term residents or latecomers on the Little Tennessee River. It is now clear that they were latecomers, and I think it fair to say that these few words from a Spanish document have done more to settle the controversy than archaeological research could ever have done.[31]

By concentrating on the interior of the Southeast, I do not mean to imply that nothing remains to be done on the history of what might be called Spanish Florida proper (the area of the administrative centers and missions of Florida, Georgia, and South Carolina). This, after all, is the only area of the Southeast where there is a continuous historical record for the entire period from 1565 to 1670. It is quite outside my competence to review work in this area, and even if it were not, I doubt that I would be able to improve on Michael Scardaville's recent review of this literature.[32] I do, however, want to reiterate that the experience of Indians in Spanish Florida proper was quite different from that of Indians in the interior and that the task of writing their history is correspondingly different.[33]

In conclusion, I would like to make two confessions that carry with them recommendations that are especially meant for young scholars who are just beginning their research. My first confession is that despite the title of my paper, I have always thought that conceiving of the early Southeast as a "Spanish borderlands" was unfortunate. Such a conception leads one to think that what was most important about the Southeast in the sixteenth and seventeenth centuries is that it lay on the outermost fringe of the Spanish Empire in the New World. This ignores the fact that the Southeast was the domain of indigenous societies whose ancestors had arrived over ten thousand years earlier. Moreover, these societies underwent a profound historical transformation in the wake of Spanish exploration. I am aware that Spanish borderlands history was conceived as a corrective to the biases of Anglo-American historians. But writing history from a Spanish point of view as opposed to an Anglo point of view serves history no better than ethnohistorians who attempt to write history from an Indian point of view. Our task should be to reconstruct the early history of the South taking pains to reveal the structural factors that were peculiar to the region. Our aim should be to write what the *Annaliste* historians call "total history." Such a history should have a full cast of faithfully drawn characters—Indians, Spaniards, French, and English—and these characters should be placed in the context of the slow-moving structural features that have shaped human experience in this region. Furthermore, it should be a history that pays as much attention to the mundane particulars of everyday life as to the more vivid events of history.[34]

The history of the sixteenth- and seventeenth-century South seems to be an ideal subject for interdisciplinary research. I would be the first to say that what little insight I have been able to acquire has come through the interdisciplinary cooperation of archaeologists, historians of Spanish America, geographers, and linguists. But my second confession is that I do not believe that interdisciplinary research will lead to the truly fundamental historical formulations that are needed. All too often, it seems to me, interdisciplinary research explores *x* number of facets of a problem but never quite gets at the crystalline structure of the problem itself.

It is my conviction that the truly fundamental formulations of the history of the early South will be established by historians who are willing to make excursions into such sister disciplines as archaeology, anthropology, comparative sociology, geography, ecology, and so on, as well as to master the necessary languages: Spanish, French, and at least a structural knowledge of some of the major Indian languages. This is a tall order, and this is why I have specifically addressed my concluding remarks to young scholars. Again, for inspiration I recommend to them the works of the progeny of Marc Bloch, who have not hesitated to borrow from allied social sciences what was useful to them, and history has been much the gainer.

NOTES

1. Charles Hudson, "The Crucial Problem in the Ethnohistory of the Southeast," paper presented at the annual meeting of the Southern Anthropological Society, Lexington, KY, 1978.

2. Charles Hudson, "An Unknown South: Spanish Explorers and Southeastern Chiefdoms," in George Sabo III and William M. Schneider, eds., *Visions and Revisions: Ethnohistoric Perspectives on Southern Cultures,* Proceedings of the Southern Anthropological Society No. 20 (Athens: University of Georgia Press, 1987), pp. 6-24; Charles Hudson and Carmen McClendon, eds., "The Forgotten Centuries: Europeans and Indians in the American South, 1513-1704," unpublished.

3. Robert Silverberg, *Mound Builders of Ancient America: The Archaeology of a Myth* (Greenwich, CT: New York Graphic Society, 1968).

4. Erich von Daniken, *Chariots of the Gods* (New York: G. P. Dutton, 1970).

5. Gordon R. Willey and Jeremy A. Sabloff, *A History of American Archaeology* (London: Thames and Hudson, 1974), pp. 36-38.

6. Charles Colcock Jones, Jr., *Antiquities of the Southern Indians* (New York: Appleton and Company, 1873).

7. Cyrus Thomas, *The Mound Explorations of the Bureau of American Ethnology, Twelfth Annual Report, 1890-91* (Washington, DC: GPO, 1891).

8. René Loudonniere, *Three Voyages,* trans. Charles E. Bennett (Gainesville: University of Florida Press, 1975).

9. E.g., A. S. Le Page du Pratz, *The History of Louisiana,* ed. Joseph G. Tregle, Jr. (Baton Rouge: Louisiana State University Press, 1975); James Adair, *The History of the American Indians* (1775); Bernard Romans, *A Concise Natural History of East and West Florida* (1775).

10. Bruce Smith, Vincas Steponaitis, Dan Morse, and Phyllis Morse.

11. Charles Francis Bannon, *Spanish Borderlands Frontier, 1513-1821* (New York: Holt, Rhinehart, and Winston, 1963), pp. 31, 47.

12. John R. Swanton, *Final Report of the United States De Soto Expedition Commission* (Washington, DC: Smithsonian Institution Press, 1985), pp. 343c-43d (first published in 1939).

13. Paul Hoffman has recently prepared a new translation of this document.

14. Chester DePratter, Charles Hudson, and Marvin Smith, "Juan Pardo's Explorations in the Interior Southeast, 1566-1568," *Florida Historical Quarterly* 62 (1983): 125-158; Charles Hudson, "Juan Pardo's Excursion Beyond Chiaha," *Tennessee Anthropologist* 12 (1987): 74-87.

15. Charles R. Ewen, "Soldier of Fortune: Hernando de Soto in the Territory of the Apalachee, 1539-1540," in David Hurst Thomas, ed., *Columbian Consequences* (Washington, DC: Smithsonian Institution Press, 1990), 2:83-91.

16. Charles Hudson, Marvin Smith, and Chester DePratter, "The Hernando de Soto Expedition: from Apalachee to Chiaha," *Southeastern Archaeology* 3 (1984): 65-77.

17. Chester DePratter, Charles Hudson, and Marvin Smith, "The Hernando de Soto Expedition: From Chiaha to Mabila," in Reid R. Badger and Lawrence A. Clayton, eds.,

Alabama and the Borderlands: From Prehistory to Statehood (University, AL: University of Alabama Press, 1985), pp. 108–26.

18. Charles Hudson, "The Hernando de Soto Expedition: the Landing," presented at the annual meeting of the American Society for Ethnohistory," New Orleans, LA, 1985; Charles Hudson and Jerald Milanich, "Hernando de Soto and the Indians of Florida," unpublished; Charles Hudson, Marvin Smith, and Chester DePratter, "The Hernando de Soto Expedition: From Mabila to the Mississippi River," in David H. Dye and Cheryl Anne Cox, *Towns and Temples Along the Mississippi* (Tuscaloosa: University of Alabama Press, 1990), pp. 181–207; Charles Hudson, "De Soto in Arkansas: A Brief Synopsis," *Field Notes: Newsletter of the Arkansas Archaeological Society*, no. 205 (July/August 1985): 3–12.

19. Charles Hudson, Marvin Smith, Chester DePratter, and Emilia Kelley, "The Tristán de Luna Expedition, 1559–1561," *Southeastern Archaeology* 8 (1989): 31–45; Charles Hudson, "A Spanish-Coosa Alliance in Sixteenth-Century North Georgia," *Georgia Historical Quarterly* 62 (1988): 599–626.

20. See, e.g., C. Clifford Boyd, Jr., and Gerald F. Schroedl, "In Search of Coosa," *American Antiquity* 52 (1987): 840–44, and Charles Hudson, Marvin Smith, David Hally, Richard Polhemus, and Chester DePratter, "Reply to Boyd and Schroedl," *American Antiquity* 52 (1987: 845–56).

21. Charles Hudson, *The Juan Pardo Expeditions: Exploration of the Carolinas and Tennessee, 1566–1568* (Washington, DC: Smithsonian Institution Press, 1990), pp. 51–112.

22. Charles Hudson, "The Social Context of the Chiefdom of Ichisi," presented at the Ocmulgee Conference, Macon, GA, November 1986; Mark Williams, "Growth and Decline of the Oconee Province," in Hudson and McClendon, eds., "Forgotton Centuries."

23. David G. Anderson, "Political Change in Chiefdom Societies: Cycling in the Late Prehistoric Southeastern United States" (Ph.D. diss., University of Michigan, 1990).

24. Not all agree with this analysis. See Chester B. DePratter, "Cofitachequi: Ethnohistorical and Archaeological Evidence, " in Albert C. Goodyear and Glen T. Hanson, eds., *Studies in South Carolina Archaeology,* Anthropological Studies 9 (South Carolina Institute of Archaeology and Anthropology, 1989), pp. 133–56.

25. Karen Booker, Charles Hudson, and Robert Rankin, "Multilingualism in Two Paramount Chiefdoms in the Sixteenth-Century Southeastern United States," unpublished.

26. Ibid.

27. Charles Hudson, Marvin Smith, David Hally, Richard Polhemus, and Chester DePratter, "Coosa: A Chiefdom in the Sixteenth-century Southeastern United States," *American Antiquity* 50 (1985): 723–37.

28. Charles Hudson, "Early Social History of the Southeastern Indians," presented at the symposium "Native Peoples of the Southeastern United States: A Retrospective Occasioned by the Sesquicentennial of the Great Removal," Tallahassee, FL, March 5, 1987.

29. Marvin Smith, *Archaeology of Aboriginal Culture Change in the Interior Southeast: Depopulation during the Early Historic Period* (Gainesville: University of Florida Press, 1987).

30. See Hudson and McClendon, "Forgotten Centuries."

31. Hudson, "Juan Pardo's Excursion Beyond Chiaha."

32. Michael C. Scardaville, "Approaches to the Study of the Southeastern Borderlands," in R. Reid Badger and Lawrence A. Clayton, eds., *Alabama and the Borderlands: From Prehistory to Statehood* (University, AL: University of Alabama Press, 1985), pp. 184–96.

33. See, in particular, recent publications by John H. Mann, *Apalachee: The Land Between the Rivers* (Gainesville: University of Florida Press, 1988), and John H. Mann, "Summary Guide to Spanish Florida Missions and *Visitas,*" *The Americas* 56 (1990): 417–513.

34. Fernand Braudel, *On History* (Chicago: University of Chicago Press, 1980), trans. Sarah Matthews.

JOHN L. KESSELL

9. Research in the Western Spanish Borderlands

On-Site and Out-of-Sight

This chapter simply did not come together as I had hoped it would. I found myself perplexed instead of inspired. There were several reasons, all related, it would seem, to exclusivity.

First, considering the purpose of this conference—"how to identify and copy materials abroad related to the Hispanic experience in the United States," in the words of the letter we all received—I was struck by how one-sided it seemed. Although I am certain that no member of the Christopher Columbus Quincentenary Jubilee Commission intended that it be so, our "national initiative" to gain access to records of the Spanish heritage of the United States sounds like documentary manifest destiny. Certainly we should be as committed collectively—as I know we are individually—to making our own records as accessible to others as we want theirs to be to us. Anyway we should, in the interest of better understanding, say so.

Perhaps unprecedented, multilateral archival sharing does lie ahead in the next half-millennium. Driven by well-intentioned desires to preserve and make accessible digitally our common documentary heritage, I wonder if we will go too far. I already know that I do not want to come back in the year 2492 as an exclusively computerized historian.

Picture it. Images of all the documents, not only those that used to be in the Archivo General de Indias (AGI) in Seville and the archive of the Museo Naval in Madrid, but also those in the Archivo de Notrías in Torrelaguna, the parish archive of Huéscar, and the family archive of the Duques de Albuquerque in Cuéllar—all are now "captured" digitally on laser disks, fully and instantly accessible, along with detailed finding aids, even to Indiferente General.

In front of a thousand screens in antiseptic pods at libraries from College Park to Las Cruces, they sit, hunched ergonomically, pale researchers keying in Demography/Censuses/New Mexico/Santa Cruz de la Cañada/1650–1750/enter. Seven interminable seconds later, down scroll lists for selection, viewing in facsimile, graphic enhancement, and printing. Add to this the comfort of knowing that somewhere, in a cavernous, hermetically sealed crypt in the Valle de los Caídos, lie the originals, quiet and undisturbed.

Some years ago, I anticipated the brave new world of archival research at arm's length—or, as I have chosen to call it, out-of-sight—in the then essentially noncomputerized environment of a polished office building in Salt Lake City. There, in the Genealogical Library of the Church of Jesus Christ of the Latter-day Saints, I consulted microfilm of the baptismal register from the Asunción Sagrario Parish for the 1680s. It was all wonderfully convenient. I did not have to justify and cover the cost of international travel. There was little threat of earthquake or strike or unanticipated religious holiday. I could drink the water. I did not have to go to Mexico City.

Digitization puts in our hands the mixed blessing of out-of-sight, electronic access. I guess what scares and perplexes me is the prospect of isolation and impersonality, of historical research removed from its cultural context. There is too much to lose: those qualities someone who has walked the streets, met descendants, and experienced the culture brings to the writing of history.

At least from time to time, I want to go to Mexico or Spain, to follow the archival trail, to work on my Spanish, and to deal with Mexicans and Spaniards. There is something too, a mystical transfer perhaps, or simply an appreciation or respect, that comes from handling the documents themselves. That human element—whatever the actual, written artifact might have to say to us—fades on microfilm or in computer-generated image. Surely future generations of researchers will want some access to what originals survive. I hope technology will supply new ways of conserving old paper.

Meanwhile, digitizing the documents to preserve their images and the information they contain, while decreasing the random need to handle them, is an encouraging prospect. Sadly, documents are not forever. I admit to grimacing at the sight of the cord cutting deeper into the margins as I strained to get a three-foot-tall legajo back together under the critical gaze of the porteros at the Archivo General de Simancas. And just to have fotocopias en el acto of documents I needed in my own personal research, I have looked the other way as the willing employee of a notarial archive further cracked the spine of a fat protocolo, slamming it open-faced onto the glass while tiny pieces of three-hundred-year-old paper fell to the floor.

In the western Spanish borderlands, today's champion of digitization, Charles W. Polzer, looks to preservation of archival materials on a grand scale. At the same time, through the Documentary Relations of the Southwest Project at the University of Arizona (DRSW), launched by him in 1975, Polzer advocates accessibility. An ambitious team effort, the DRSW produces computerized finding aids and documentary publications as avenues into the mass of primary sources for the entire region between the 22nd and 38th parallels of north latitude and the 92nd and 123rd meridians of west longitude throughout the colonial period.

The DRSW is amassing a data base of vital information extracted from broadly selected, documentary materials in the archives of the United States, Spain, and Mexico. With the recent incorporation of data from the entire Provincias Internas section of the Archivo General de la Nacion (AGN) in Mexico City, it now contains some 30,000 main entires. The key to this teeming data bank is a master annotated bibliography of primary sources published in increments and available as computer printout or on microfiche, with indexes of places, persons, ethnic groups, key terms, general subjects, and archives.

Using these research tools of their own making, the DRSW staff has fashioned and brought forth *The Presido and Militia on the Northern Frontier of New Spain: A Documentary History, Volume One: 1570–1700,* and *Pedro de Rivera and the Military Regulations for Northern New Spain, 1724–1729,* the first two of the project's promised full-length publications.[1] Selected and annotated documents, presented in English translation and modernized Spanish transcript, reveal not only the evolution of the frontier military during a little-known period but also myriad details of interest to ethnologists, social historians, students of material culture, and others.

By the time of this meeting, if I am not mistaken, the entire DRSW data bank will be on line, accessible by full text search, and demonstrable nearby at Advanced Projects International on a single 5 1/4-in. laser disk. Integrating the DRSW finding aids and the digitally captured documents themselves is, of course, the next step.

In the case of colonial New Mexico, we have had access to copies of the documents for three generations. Beginning in the early predigital era before the turn of present century, Adolph F. Bandelier, and later Fanny R. Bandelier, Lansing B. Bloom, France V. Scholes, and George P. Hammond—

sponsored by the Archaeological Institute of America, Peabody Museum, Carnegie Institution, Library of Congress, and others—acquired thousands of pages of transcripts and photoreproductions from the Spanish Archives of New Mexico (SANM), the Historia and Provincias Internas sections of the AGN, and the Audiencias of Mexico and Guadalajara in the AGI.

Here then, collected long ago and not yet thoroughly studied, is much of the documentation for the New World part of our story, arguably, to us, the more important part. What we have not had, and still do not to a large degree, is material for the Old World part of the story. Our more-or-less exclusive focus on the Americas is perhaps best illustrated in the context of the Vargas Project at the University of New Mexico, of which Rick Hendricks and I are editors.

A long-term, documentary editing venture, the Vargas Project seeks to make more readily available the primary source material for the pivotal period of New Mexico's recolonization in the 1690s, when the Spanish Crown's justification for further subsidizing the colony shifted from mainly missionary, as it had been for much of the seventeenth century, to mainly military, as it would be throughout the eighteenth and into the nineteenth century.

We look toward publishing a seven-volume, scholarly edition in English translation of the journals of don Diego de Vargas, 1691–1704—in effect, the principal archives of the era—accompanied by microfiche of the Spanish transcripts. With the help and encouragement of John J. Nitti of the Dictionary of the Old Spanish Language Project at the University of Wisconsin, Madison, we are adapting the computer methodology set forth in David Mackenzie's *A Manual of Manuscript Transcription for the Dictionary of the Old Spanish Language* to enable linguistic analysis of the text.[2]

Our unanticipated initial volume, a prefatory biographical work entitled *Remote Beyond Compare: Letters of don Diego de Vargas to His Family from New Spain and New Mexico, 1675–1706* resulted from the generous access granted by Vargas descendants to two private archives in Madrid.[3] Not surprisingly, the personal correspondence of this middle-ranking royal official in the waning Hapsburg years presents him in a much more human light than does the public record. Yet he is not a chronicler of the Spanish Indies. Although he is immensely and pragmatically interested in his New World surroundings—as the journals will show—Vargas sees little reason to share that interest with his relatives in Spain. The remaining six volumes, in contrast, will focus on the process of recolonization. They are to follow, *mediante el favor divino*, in the 1990s.

The desirability of complementary Old World materials is, I suspect, as obvious for other places and times as it is for New Mexico during the recolonization. Vargas and a number of his associates were born and spent their formative years in Spain; he, at least, never gave up the hope of an honorable return.

The challenge of Spanish roots in search of documentation and the response of a Columbus Quincentenary national initiative to identify documents for copying seem happily compatible. But are they? How do we target beforehand what we want? Without more personal, on-site research, I find myself singularly unprepared to make a wish list of specific documents, legajos, or archives to have copied or digitized abroad. With the exception of certain well-known entire repositories or sections thereof, the documents are so scattered as to defy orderly grouping, yet so interrelated that the researcher can rarely predict where the trail will lead. Archives in Madrid yield clues to documents in Valladolid, Cádiz, Granada, Simancas, and elsewhere. Until I went to Madrid, I had no idea that any of Vargas's personal correspondence had survived.

As a reward for his restoration of New Mexico, Diego de Vargas was entitled in 1698 the first Marqués de la Nava de Barcinas. A listing of the Spanish nobility today revealed that the title was current and that the present holder, the twelfth marquess, lived in Madrid. He agreed to receive me. As we talked, I could not keep my eyes off a large, glass-fronted bookcase visible in the adjoining room. It was full of printed books, part of the eighteenth-century library of the Conde de Campomanes, as well as bundles of documents. It could be, the marquess allowed, that the collection contained something about Diego de Vargas and New Mexico.

Kindly arranging for daily visits, the marquess permitted me to go through this private archive. I did not expect to find anything new bearing on New Mexico among the printed works. The first two bundles of documents proved to be nineteenth-century financial records of a family holding in the province of Badajoz. The third looked identical. At least I would know what was not here. Untying the cord and laying back the board, I nearly fell off the chair. Someone had written in an elegant hand across a blank sheet of paper "Correspondencia de d. Diego de Vargas."

Here were twenty-five personal letters, mostly by Vargas, some in his own unstudied scrawl, written from Tlalpujahua, Mexico City, El Paso, and Sante Fe. There was not time to transcribe them. Besides, there were hundreds of manuscript pages dealing with the family and its titles. Might I have them microfilmed? The marquess was sympathetic but wanted others in the family to concur. At a gathering of the clan, after my halting but earnest presentation, the consensus was favorable.

The following spring, a similar thing happened. The trail this time led from the Fundación Universitaria Española in Madrid, through a politically exiled Uruguayan ex-senator and a deceased Spanish diplomat, to another branch of the family. Evidently, a generation or two back, two (or perhaps more) members divided up the family archive. "Here, you take this one; I'll take that one." With this second find, the total of Vargas letters and other family documents doubled. Surely there are more.

As part of our national initiative, why should we not invest as much in facilitating research visits by scholars of all the interested countries as in copying documents? Also, in addition to wish lists of archival material to copy—the general: all the protocolos for Cádiz and the Puerto de Santa María, since they were points of departure and return; or the particular: only the protocolos for 1672–73 because Vargas spent six months at that time waiting in Cadiz for a dispatch boat to sail—I would like to see an updated, expanded, and computerized version of Lino Gómez Canedo's two-volume *Los archivos de la historia de América: Período colonial español.*[4]

As researchers, we simply cannot know too much about Spanish administrative and archival history. How, when, and for what purpose was this archive created? What policy changes, jurisdictional shifts, and calamities have affected it over the years? How are documents here related to documents in other archives? Where did the secret archive of the Council of the Orders end up, what manner of documentation does it contain, and has it been cataloged?

Why not then a Columbian-world, superarchival inventory incorporating existing computer programs (like PIC in Spain) and the kinds of information compiled in Henry Putney Beers, *Spanish and Mexican Records of the American Southwest: A Bibliographical Guide to Archive and Manuscript Sources;* Richard E. Greenleaf and Michael C. Meyer, *Research in Mexican History: Topics, Methodology, Sources, and a Practical Guide to Field Research;* and the *Guía de fuentes para la historia de Ibero-América conservadas en España?*[5]

In conclusion, let me mention another very good if obvious reason for supporting on-site research as part of our national initiative during and after the Quincentenary—international goodwill. In Spain recently, Rick Hendricks and I wanted to find out more about don Pedro Rodríguez Cubero, who succeeded Diego de Vargas in office in 1697. When the arrogant Vargas allegedly sought to obstruct his successor's administration, Rodríguez Cubero locked him up for nearly three years. As a belated consequence, don Pedro, despite growing evidence to the contrary, is reviled in New Mexico today as a jealous and vindictive incompetent.

Two years before, in Mexico City, we had learned that Rodríguez Cubero was from Huéscar in southern Spain, not from Calatayud in the north, as had been previously thought. In Huéscar we hoped to find the date of his birth and whatever else we could about his family. Three hours north of Granada in a basin-and-range setting that reminded us of New Mexico, Huéscar still serves as a regional commercial and agricultural center. The mayor and town council turned out to meet us and accompany us to the parish archive. There we found the record of don Pedro's birth, his parents' marriage, and other vital data.

What is more, in Huéscar we found enthusiastic interest in the Spanish Indies. The people are fascinated that a son of the pueblo went on to govern in America. They want to name a street in his honor. They want to maintain contact with us. They propose that the best way to commemorate the Quincentenary is through people-to-people sharing of the bonds that unite Old World and New. The toast we heard repeated as we took our leave was "1992 began today in Huéscar!"

I would urge only that we remember, in this climate of laser disks and national initiatives, that personal, on-site research—as long as we enjoy friendly relations with the other countries of the Columbian world—will remain as an honorable, satisfying, and eminently worthwhile complement, perhaps for several centenaries to come.

NOTES

   1. Both comp. and ed. Thomas H. Naylor and Charles W. Polzer (Tucson: University of Arizona Press, 1986 and 1988).
   2. (Madison: Hispanic Seminar of Medieval Studies, 1986).
   3. (Albuquerque: University of New Mexico Press, 1989).
   4. (Mexico City: Instituto Panamericano de Geografía e Historia, 1961).
   5. (Tucson: University of Arizona Press, 1979); (Lincoln: University of Nebraska Press, 1973); 2 vols. (Madrid: Dirección General de Archivos y Bibliotecas, 1966–69).

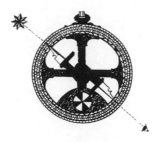

3 · Projects

Introduction to Part 3

William Coker takes us through the search for the documents to tell properly the story of merchants in the Southeast of the late eighteenth and early nineteenth centuries as dominion and sovereignty changed rapidly in the area among English, Spaniards, French, and the johnny-come-lately Americans. It was a confusing period, but Coker and his colleagues focused narrowly on the premier merchants of the period, and this tight focus has produced one of the most significant collections of the Hispanic period in the Southeast when borders seemed to be in a state of constant fluctuation.

Paul Hoffman shows us how another state—Louisiana—has gone about accumulating the documents of its early Spanish period. It is a story of frustration and triumph, of dealing with bureaucrats and changing times, and one ultimately of persistence and success. Hoffman draws attention to the vast Spanish background of greater Louisiana's history, one that can be so richly sensed in the streets of New Orleans and that has been enriched by the efforts of Hoffman and his predecessors and contemporaries.

Charles Polzer's essay is the song of a man committed to a vision called the New World Archive. Every movement has its prophets and its realists, its dreamers and its dogmatists. Father Polzer stretches his reach across these domains, and his all-encompassing vision and his quest for an all-inclusive preservation suffuse his essay with wit and dedication.

Hernando de Soto's famed expedition into the Southeast between 1539 and 1543 is the focus of Douglas Jones's interest. His chapter tells why Alabamians in general, but archaeologists, ethnographers, and historians in particular, have focused tightly on the Soto *entrada* that produced such havoc among the native American population and so little lucre for the conquistadors. The need for ready access to the invaluable Spanish documentation of the period reinforces the same need expressed by Charles Hudson.

Michael Scardaville briefly describes the creation and evolution of the Southeastern Columbus Quincentennial Commission. It is a regional organization dedicated to properly commemorating the Quincentennial by bringing together many groups, such as the State Humanities Councils of ten states, to plan and focus activities across the Southeast. One of their many goals is to foster scholarly activities, such as the preparation of a guide to Latin American and Hispanic manuscript collections, to take the short-term enthusiasm of the Quincentennial fever, and translate it into long-term benefits for both the scholarly and public community interested in our Hispanic and Latin American history and heritage.

WILLIAM S. COKER

10. Indian Traders of the Southeastern Spanish Borderlands

A Spanish, French, and English Documentary Project

The purpose of this chapter is to call attention to the Indian trading firm of Panton, Leslie & Company and its successor firm, John Forbes & Company, and to detail within limits the documentary sources that comprise the collection known as "The Papers of Panton, Leslie & Company."

The article is divided into several parts: a historical overview of the two trading companies; the origin of the documentary project, "The Papers of Panton, Leslie & Company"; the major collections of documents that formed the nucleus of "The Papers of Panton, Leslie & Company" with some information about those collections that contained significant numbers of documents from the Spanish and Cuban archives; the documents collected during the project from the various Spanish, French, and British archives and libraries; and the two major accomplishments of the project; the microfilming and marketing of "The Papers of Panton, Leslie & Company," and the narrative history of the companies published in 1986.

The five original partners of Panton, Leslie & Company, formed at St. Augustine, British East Florida, in late 1782 or early 1783, were William Panton, Thomas Forbes, John Leslie, William Alexander, and Charles McLatchy. All were Scotsmen engaged in trade with the colonists and Indians of South Carolina, Georgia, and East Florida prior to and during the American Revolution. Contrary to many of their friends and neighbors in South Carolina and Georgia, they maintained their loyalty to Great Britain. It was a very practical matter for them as most of their trade goods, especially gunpowder, lead, and guns, came from Great Britain. To have become colonial patriots, or rebels to the British cause, would have ended their supply of such materials. As good Scots and businessmen they did not wish to kill the goose that laid their golden eggs. Their Loyalist stand eventually forced all of them to take residence in East Florida, one of several British mainland colonies that remained faithful to the motherland. There, through the influence of Governor Patrick Tonyn and others, they managed to continue in the mercantile business and, in 1783, received a license for the Creek trade. The company had several trading posts on the St. Johns River, and in 1783 established a store on the Wakulla River, near San Marcos de Apalache, several hundred miles west of St. Augustine.

When word finally arrived that East and West Florida were to be returned to Spain, the partners were dismayed but not defeated. John Leslie, who would take charge of the firm's St. Augustine branch, quickly befriended the newly arrived Spanish governor, Vincente Manuel de Zéspedes, by supplying him with Indian goods and presents, items that Zéspedes did not bring with him. The governor became a firm supporter of the company and strongly endorsed its petition to remain in the Floridas under Spanish auspices. Because Spain had neither the desired trade goods nor traders with experience in this particular Indian trade, it permitted the company and several of the partners to remain until such time as Spanish traders could replace them. That time never arrived.

The company's move into the West Florida Indian trade was facilitated by the misfortunes of Gilberto Antonio de St. Maxent and the firm of Mather and Strother. But Panton also gained the support of Alexander McGillivray, the prominent Creek headman, and of the governor and intendant of Louisiana and West Florida, Esteban Miró and Martín Navarro, respectively. All three of them received a percentage of the company's profits. By 1785, Panton had officially opened a trading post at Panzacola (Pensacola), and others soon followed: Mobile, Chickasaw Bluffs (Memphis), Prospect Bluff on the Appalachicola River, Bon Secour on Mobile Bay, and New Orleans. The company slowly but surely secured a near monopoly of southern Indian trade: Muscogulges (Creeks and Seminoles), Cherokees, Chickasaws, and Chocktaws.[1]

The one thing that worked to the company's advantage and the Indians' disadvantage was the extension of credit to the Indians. By 1797, the southern Indians owed the company some $200,000, and for the next seventeen years Panton and his successor, John Forbes, devoted much of their time attempting to collect this huge outstanding indebtedness. Panton died in 1801, and John Forbes took his place. Forbes soon managed to secure a grant in excess of 1.4 million acres of land in West Florida, which canceled $66,533.05 of the Creek debt. Then, because Forbes realized the necessity of working with the United States, he and his associates helped to secure nearly 8 million acres of land desired by the United States from the southern Indians. In turn, the money paid the Indians for their lands was used to pay the remaining indebtedness to the company. To be sure, the company encountered many problems before the debts were finally resolved. In particular, the Indians pretended not to understand the payment of interest on their debts. This helped delay the final settlement until 1814.

Following Panton's death in 1801, the new company worked with both Spain and the United States in order to maintain the Indian trade. Several wars including the War of 1812 and the First Seminole War, 1816–18, had serious repercussions on the company and its relations with the Indians.[2]

After 1815, the company restricted its trade largely to Pensacola and Mobile, although it continued to maintain Indian trading posts on the Appalachicola and at San Marcos de Apalache (St. Marks) until after 1821.[3] Now let us turn to a brief history of the documentary project, "The Papers of Panton, Leslie & Company."

In 1972 the University of West Florida approved a recommendation by Coker and the director of libraries, James A. Services, to collect all the papers pertaining to the companies just described. By 1973, the Florida Historical Society and the University of Florida had joined in the project. That same year, the National Historical Publications and Records Commission agreed to provide funding for the collection phase. But others had already collected many hundreds of pages of documents on the same subject. Thus the first effort was to secure copies of the seven major collections that would form the nucleus of "The Papers of Panton, Leslie and Company."[4]

In 1921, John Batterson Stetson, Jr., undertook the earliest documentary project of note for Florida history. He enlisted the help of Jeannette Thurber Connor and Irene A. Wright, and eventually they collected some 7,000 documents (circa 130,000 sheets) from the Archivo General de Indias in Seville, Spain, pertaining to Florida history. In 1954, the P. K. Yonge Library of Florida History, University of Florida, Gainesville, acquired the Stetson Collection.[5] The Stetson Collection has recently been calendared and the calendar is available on microfilm from the P. K. Yonge Library of Florida History. Some documents from this collection are included in the Papers of Panton, Leslie & Company, but the documentary history of the company was not the primary objective of the Stetson Collection effort.

First among those to accept the challenge of collecting the papers, and one who planned to write a comprehensive history of the companies, was Elizabeth Howard West, a noted Texas librarian. Miss West discussed the project with Professor Frederick Jackson Turner, who believed "it would be an excellent project."[6] Beginning her work in the early 1930s, Miss West traveled to Havana and secured a number of pertinent documents there. Subsequently, she went to Spain and acquired many more useful documents from the Spanish archives.[7]

Another person who also secured many documents pertaining to the Panton and Forbes companies from the Spanish archives was Professor David Hart White. A member of the history faculty of the University of Alabama at Birmingham, White was working on the history of John Forbes and Company and a biography of Governor Vicente Folch y Juan. Folch served in Spanish West Florida for a number of years and was governor of the colony from 1796 to 1811. Folch had intimate connections with both the Panton and Forbes companies. Several years before he died, Dr. White donated a microfilm copy of his papers to the project. Plans also called for White to assist in writing the narrative history of the companies, but he passed away before that could be accomplished.

Two descendants of John Innerarity, Marie Taylor Greenslade and Heloise Cruzat, also collected many documents pertaining to the two companies.[8] Innerarity, a nephew of William Panton, came to Pensacola in 1802 and eventually headed the local branch of John Forbes & Company. Over a period of years, the *Florida Historical Quarterly* published a number of the Greenslade documents. These two valuable collections, the Greenslade and Cruzat papers, are now on file in the Florida Historical Society Collection at the University of South Florida Library, Tampa. Although many of the documents in both these collections are in Spanish, neither Greenslade nor Cruzat visited the Spanish archives. The documents apparently came from the papers of John Innerarity, his brother James, and John Forbes.

Another collection of considerable value to the project was the John Forbes Papers in the Mobile Public Library, Mobile, Alabama. The library purchased this collection from Heartman's, a New Orleans manuscript and book dealer, in 1953.[9] In 1967, the Archives Department of Auburn University Library became interested in the Forbes Papers. Carolyn J. Dixon calendared the collection which was then microfilmed. A significant number of the documents in this collection are also in Spanish.

Three collections in the Middleton Library at Louisiana State University,

Baton Rouge, the James Innerarity, John Innerarity, and Henry Wilson papers, proved to be extremely valuable additions to the project collection. John Innerarity's brother James, who came to West Florida in 1796, headed the Mobile branch of the Panton and Forbes companies. Colonel Henry Wilson was John Innerarity's son-in-law. Louisiana State University acquired these collections from several dealers. It purchased the Wilson Papers in 1939 and the James and John Innerarity Papers in 1954.[10] A few of the papers in the John and James Innerarity Papers are in Spanish.

The one major in-house collection of documents at the University of West Florida, which provided the initial inspiration for the Panton, Leslie Project, was the Innerarity-Hulse Papers. Dr. Isaac Hulse, a U.S. Navy medical officer stationed at the Pensacola Navy Yard, was John Innerarity's son-in-law. Francis Taylor, a descendant of John Innerarity, deposited the papers in the Special Collections Department of the John C. Pace Library, University of West Florida, Pensacola. Several years ago, Mr. Taylor related to the author that early in World War II while he was at Casablanca in North Africa, he had met a priest (whose name he did not remember) who told him that he had written a history of Panton, Leslie and Company. Mr. Taylor had met Father Paul Edward (Roderick) Wheeler, O.F.M., a distinguished Franciscan scholar and first editor of *The Americas*. Indeed, Father Wheeler had completed his doctoral dissertation on Panton, Leslie and Company at the University of Madrid in 1940.[11] In fact, it was the first dissertation ever written on the subject. Father Wheeler's dissertation, as well as several other dissertations and master's theses written at the University of Madrid on the company or upon related subjects, are in the author's possession. In the preparation of their studies, they relied primarily upon documents from the Spanish archives, which served as an invaluable source for locating documents in Spain.

With the acquisition of copies of the documents from the foregoing collections, each document was calendared and integrated into a chronological file. The documents are identified by collection (Forbes, Stetson, West, White, or other) and also by the archive, section, and legajo (bundle) number if obtained from the Spanish archives, or with appropriate identification if secured elsewhere. The various guides to the collection are discussed below.

In 1973, and periodically for the next several years, the author made extended research trips to Spain, France, England, Scotland, Mexico, and Canada and visited the major archives and libraries in those countries to secure copies of additional documents. Likewise, all the appropriate archives and libraries in the United States were visited, if there was any promise that they had documents of interest to the project. All books, journal articles, and other sources were screened for documents. Occasionally pertinent published documents were discovered that, for whatever reason, had not been collected elsewhere. For example, the East Tennessee Historical Society Publications beginning with volume 9 (1937) contains translations of a number of documents that Duvon C. Corbitt acquired in Cuba.

When the collection phase was over, 517 reels of microfilm had been acquired. Of the thousands of documents collected, 8,357 concerned the Panton and Forbes companies. The other documents pertained to the history of East and West Florida generally. Each document ranged from one to several hundred pages in length. There is a general guide to the 517 reels of microfilm, which is on file in the Special Collections Department, John C. Pace Library, University of West Florida, Pensacola.

There are two guides to the 8,357 documents selected for microfilming. Several years ago, Tamara West Harrell compiled a general subject guide comprised of copies of the calendars (3×5 cards) of the documents arranged by subject matter. This guide has not been microfilmed or otherwise published, but it is available in the Special Collections Department, John C. Pace Library. The other guide is a part of the microfilm edition of the Panton, Leslie and John Forbes Papers and will be discussed in that context.

In 1986, Research Publications, Incorporated, microfilmed the 8,357 documents selected from the general collection. This effort produced twenty-six reels of microfilm. The company also prepared a guide, *The Papers of Panton, Leslie and Company: Guide to the Microfilm Collection.*[12] The guide includes an Introduction (pp. v–vi), which is a condensation of some of the material in this chapter. The guide also has sections on "Arrangement and Usage" (p. vii) and "Source Description" (pp. ix–xv). Then follows a "Chronological Listing" (pp. 1–667), which is the heart of the guide. Therein all documents are listed chronologically for the twenty-six reels of microfilm. Each listing contains an abstract of the subject matter with appropriate identification of the document. This listing was copied from the individual calendars of the documents prepared by the project staff at the University of West Florida. Finally, a "Name Listing" (pp. 671–764) provides an alphabetical index to the authors and addresses of the documents.[13]

In 1986, the University Presses of Florida published the narrative history of the companies: William S. Coker and Thomas D. Watson, *Indian Traders of the Southeastern Spanish Borderlands: Panton, Leslie & Company and John Forbes & Company, 1783–1847.*[14] This volume contains an in-depth history of the companies, the personalities involved, their relations with the Indians and others, and the international complexities that affected them. Although there is no definitive bibliography of the companies, the most comprehensive bibliography is in the narrative history (pp. 375–94). In May 1987, the Florida Historical Society selected the book for the Rembert W. Patrick Memorial Book Award, given for the best book on Florida history published in 1986. But the last word has not been written about these companies, and those interested are encouraged to continue the search. The documentary collection, "The Papers of Panton, Leslie & Company," is a good place to start. But the search for documents is not over yet. Several recent acquisitions deserve notice.

In the summer of 1986, an 1855 newspaper article was found, quite by accident, that gave James Innerarity credit for having warned General Andrew Jackson of the British plans to capture New Orleans before the great battle there in 1814–15. The plan originated with the cotton brokers of Liverpool, and the ultimate objective of Britain's southern campaign during the War of 1812 was the huge stockpiles of cotton and other goods on the wharves in New Orleans. Those goods were valued at some 4 million pounds sterling. One of the Liverpool cotton brokers wrote Vincent Gray, a member of the mercantile house of Antonio de Frias and Company of Havana, to inform him of the plans. Gray, a native of Massachusetts, put country before profit and wrote James Innerarity, revealing the secret. In spite of the fact that he was a native of Scotland, Innerarity, who had only been a United States citizen for about a year, warned Jackson of the British plans. This was not revealed until 1855, eight years after Innerarity's death, for fear that it might have adverse effects upon the company and its British mercantile connections.[15] This newspaper article led to the discovery of six letters in the Papers of Andrew Jackson, The Hermitage, Tennessee, written by Gray, Jackson, John Innerarity, and others, that were not in the Panton, Leslie Collection. Several of those letters originated with Gray in Havana. But there is more.

In June 1987, a Panton descendant in England, Mrs. Jean A. Vaughan, wrote the Florida State Museum in Tallahassee that she had a significant number of letters and other documents in her possession pertaining to the Panton, Leslie and Forbes companies. Not once in the fifteen-year search for company papers was there the slightest indication of the existence of these papers. On November 17, 1987, Mr. and Mrs. Vaughan visited the University of West Florida and brought with them nearly 1,600 pages of original documents. Mrs. Vaughan's grandfather collected these papers while he and other members of the family pursued claims on behalf of the Panton and Forbes heirs.[16]

One of the first letters read by this author in the Panton Family Papers, as the papers brought by the Vaughans are now called, was a letter written by William Panton in 1795. Among other things, it cleared up a little mystery that had been encountered while writing the narrative history. John Innerarity (Sr.), father of John and James Innerarity, mentioned previously, had worked at the company store on the Wakulla River near San Marcos de Apalache but returned to Pensacola about January 1793. Some two years later he left Pensacola to return to London, but no reason was ever found for his decision to leave. The Panton letter of 1795 provided the answer. "Poor Innerarity," he wrote, "got at last so very Wife sick, that I was obliged to let him go to save his life—I hope that he has got [home] safe & if he pays you a visit his Jaunt this way has furnished him with a plentiful fund for Conversation."[17]

As this is being written, the University of West Florida is in the process of purchasing these valuable papers. In the discussion with Mrs. Vaughan, she revealed that other Panton heirs, who had migrated to Canada in the nineteenth century, had also been actively engaged in pursuing claims against the companies. She believes that those descendants also had large collections of papers similar to those gathered by her grandfather. Some years ago, the author spent nearly a month in Canada searching for company papers, but no collections on the order envisioned by Mrs. Vaughan were discovered. However, the information and suggestions from her have opened up new research possibilities.

What was accomplished during the fifteen years devoted to the Papers of Panton, Leslie and Company Project? Thousands of pages of documents from numerous foreign and domestic archives and libraries were collected. With the exception of the Panton Family Papers, all the documents are available on microfilm together with a published guide. The Panton Family Papers may be examined at the Pace Library at the University of West Florida after purchase arrangements are completed. Finally the narrative history of the companies by Coker and Watson came off the press in 1986. By spring 1987, it was concluded that the project was completed, but obviously there are more materials that must be sought. Thus the search goes on; next stop Canada (again), then where?

NOTES

1. On the use of the term *Muscogulges* for the Creeks and Seminoles, see J. Leitch Wright, Jr., *Creeks and Seminoles: Destruction and Regeneration of the Muscogulge People* (Lincoln and London: University of Nebraska Press, 1986), pp. xi–xv.

2. The preceding historical sketch is condensed from William S. Coker and Thomas D. Watson, *Indian Traders of the Southeastern Spanish Borderlands: Panton, Leslie & Company and John Forbes & Company, 1783–1847* (Gainesville: University Presses of Florida, 1986).

3. Ibid., pp. 292–329.

4. Several small books and articles have been written about the documentary project. William S. Coker, *Historical Sketches of Panton, Leslie and Company* (Pensacola: University of West Florida Press, 1976), contains two essays. See also "The Papers of Panton, Leslie and Company," *Journal of the University of South Florida Library Associates* 2 (Fall 1978): 13–15; *John Forbes' Description of the Spanish Floridas, 1804* (Pensacola: Perdido Bay Press, 1979); "The Papers of Panton, Leslie and Company," in Coker and Watson, *Indian Traders,* pp. 371–74; and *The Papers of Panton, Leslie and Company: Guide to the Microfilm Collection* (Woodbridge, Ct. and Reading England: Research Publications, 1986), pp. v–vi.

5. For a history of the Stetson Collection, see Charles W. Arnade, "Florida History in Spanish Archives. Reproductions at the University of Florida," *Florida Historical Quarterly* 34 (1955): 236–50; James Alexander Robertson, "The Spanish Manuscripts of the Florida State Historical Society," *American Antiquarian Society* n.s., 34 (1929): 16–37; and "The Archival Distribution of Florida Manuscripts," *Florida Historical Quarterly* 10 (1931): 35–50.

6. Elizabeth Howard West, "The Panton, Leslie Project," copy in the West Papers, microfilm reel 4.

7. Ibid., "Work Already Completed"; Julien C. Yonge to Watt Marchman, Pensacola, March 5, 1939, copy in files of the Florida Historical Society, University of South Florida Library, Tampa, FL.

8. See ibid. for a brief discussion of the Greenslade and Cruzat papers.

9. Conversation with Mr. George Schroeter, Local History Section, Mobile Public Library, August 18, 1986. Caldwell Delaney, now director of the Museum of the City of Mobile, played a key role in the acquisition of the Forbes Papers.

10. Conversation with Mr. Robert S. Martin, assistant director of libraries for Special Collections, Louisiana State University, Baton Rouge, August 18, 1986.

11. Coker, *Historical Sketches,* p. 2. Several other theses and dissertations completed at the University of Madrid that pertained to the companies are noted in ibid.

12. (Woodbridge, CT, and Reading, England: Research Publications, 1986), xvii, 764 pp.

13. Information about the microfilm edition may be obtained by writing Research Publications, Inc., 12 Lunar Drive, Woodbridge, CT 06525.

14. (Gainesville: University Presses of Florida, 1986).

15. This was the subject of a paper read by the author at the joint meeting of the Louisiana Historical Association and the Mississippi Historical Society in New Orleans, March 13, 1987; William S. Coker, "How General Andrew Jackson Learned of the British Plans Before the Battle of New Orleans," *Gulf Coast Historical Review* 3, no. 1 (Fall 1987): 84–95.

16. Mrs. Vaughan is descended from William Panton's sister, Christian: letter of Mrs. Jean A. Vaughan to William S. Coker, Bray, Berks, England, July 24, 1987.

17. William Panton to Robert Leslie, January 1, 1793, Buckingham Smith Papers, New York Historical Society; William Panton to Alexander Smith, September 25, 1795, Panton Family Papers; see also Coker and Watson, *Indian Traders,* pp. 18–19.

PAUL E. HOFFMAN

11. The Cuban Papers Project and the National Endowment for the Humanities

The Cuban Papers Project is the second of two projects to film the major runs of Spanish materials relating to Louisiana found in the Archive of the Indies. The first was the Santo Domingo Project. Both projects originated in a speech that the Spanish ambassador to the United States made in New Orleans in 1958 during which he suggested that local institutions and scholars should pay more attention to the Spanish period in Louisiana's history. To encourage that study, he presented photographic copies of certain maps and plans from Spanish archives and intimated that the Spanish government might be receptive to a project to photocopy relevant documents. Seizing the opportunity, individuals connected with the International Trade Mart approached Loyola University to provide the scholarly expertise and to raise money.[1]

Since no one opened doors better in Franco's Spain than a Jesuit with a mission, Loyola's overtures to the Spaniards obtained the then unprecedented permission to film the Louisiana materials in entire legajos and runs of legajos. The agreement signed in 1961 limited the number of positive copies of the film and provided for the preparation and publication of a catalog of the materials filmed. Thus was born the Santo Domingo Project, whose product was a two-volume catalog edited by D. José de la Peña, then director of the Archive of the Indies, and 144 reels of microfilm of Louisiana materials found in AGI, Santo Domingo, legajos 2528–2689. The Santo Domingo Project embraced materials between 1762 and 1811.

Upon the completion of the Santo Domingo Project in 1968, the then director of the project, Rev. Dr. Charles E. O'Neill (S.J.), contemplated a continuation of the microfilming of Louisiana and West Florida materials in the more numerous legajos of the Papeles Procedentes de Cuba (PC). Nothing further was done until the mid-1970s, when he attempted to organize a consortium to fund the new project and obtained agreement in principle for it from the director of the AGI, Doña Rosario Parra. Unable to put a consortium together, O'Neill prepared a grant proposal for the National Endowment for the Humanities and submitted it for the 1975 competition under the Research Materials Program.

By this point, Dr. O'Neill and the author were in close correspondence about a possible cooperative project between Loyola and LSU. Louisiana State University agreed to provide a line item in its library budget and to work through Loyola in order to be in compliance with Louisiana's laws governing the acquisition of library materials.[2] When, therefore, the university's NEH application was not funded, we turned to developing a long-term agreement. At the same time, however, O'Neill also revised and resubmitted the NEH application, listing LSU as a party under an agreement through which LSU would provide inter-library loan service on a copy of the films. Loyola University intended that its copy of the film should be noncirculating, as was its copy of the Santo Domingo microfilms. This revised application was funded in the 1976 competition.

By the time NEH notified us that the Cuban Papers Project had been funded, O'Neill had already taken some funds held by Loyola University and begun the work of preparing the documents for microfilming. He did this because Doña Rosario Parra, director of the Archive of the Indies, had advised him in 1976 that an opportunity to have filming done would arise during 1977 and should be seized upon because another opportunity might not arise for some time. At the same time that he began the Cuban Papers Project, O'Neill was transferred from Loyola University to the directorship of the Jesuit Historical Institute in Rome. This effectively removed the director of the project from close contact with those who maintained the records of expenditures and from the shifting world of NEH operating rules. As O'Neill has commented, this arrangement did not create problems until 1980–81 for reasons that will be noted below.[3]

Independently of the Cuban Papers Project but following essentially the same methodology, the University of Southwestern Louisiana arranged for the preparation and microfilming of PC legajos 188–221, which contain much of the correspondence of the commandants of the posts, especially those of Acadiana. These materials have been incorporated into the microfilm editions prepared as part of the Cuban Papers Project.

Scope of the Project

Because of the initial need to interest Louisiana donors in the project and in light of the conditions contained in the 1961 agreement, O'Neill conceived of the Cuban Papers Project in somewhat restricted terms, taking as his principal geographic focus the present state of Louisiana and as his temporal limits 1763–1803. Certain legajos, those numbered 1–227 (Correspondence of the Governor's Office and many related items dealing with the military and treasury of the province) and 448–706 (Treasury and Intendency records), dealt mostly with the Spanish provinces of Upper and Lower Louisiana and West Florida from 1763 to 1803. If materials dating after 1803 were also included, they were to be prepared and filmed with the rest. But legajos such as PC 228–82, which dealt solely with the treasury of West Florida after 1803, were excluded from the project because they held marginal interest for the history of Baton Rouge and the "Florida parishes" of the present state of Louisiana. Similarly, the correspondence of the commandants of Pensacola and other West Florida officials dating after 1803 was not included.

In addition to including these two core groups of legajos, the project came to embrace others found in the correspondence of the captains-general of Cuba (AGI, PC 1094–2264) that were thought to be of interest for the history of the province of Louisiana. O'Neill has not stated how he applied to this part of the project the geographic and temporal sieves used to determine the core legajos, but he clearly did not do so with rigor or consistency. Thus only part of the series of legajos containing letters sent from Havana to Louisiana and West Florida were included, those for 1771–96.[4] A few additional legajos, mostly of copybooks and copies of royal *cédulas* (decrees) and treasury records that had strayed from the main body of those documents, were also included in the project.

In sum, the Cuban Papers Project consists of two cores of continuous runs of legajos, AGI, PC 1–227, and 488–706, plus 46 others that include some, but not all, of the relevant materials in the correspondence of the captains-general of Cuba. The focus is on Lower Louisiana, specifically on the area that became the state of Louisiana. Chronologically, the range is from 1762 to circa 1803. In all, some 572 actual legajos will be included in the microfilm.[5]

Unlike the Santo Domingo Papers Project, which was allowed to film materials relating only to Louisiana and excluded duplicates found in the same legajo, the Cuban Papers Project was required to prepare and film *all materials* in a given legajo, whether they dealt with Louisiana or not and whether they were duplicate, triplicate, etc., or not. In general there is little non-Louisiana–West Florida material in the legajos in question, but there is some and the project-prepared contents for each legajo reflected these inclusions.

Method

The criteria for preparing the documents for microfilming were established by Doña Rosario Parra and Dr. O'Neill in a series of conferences. They are the same criteria used in the Archive of the Indies by its staff as they prepare other parts of its vast holdings for eventual cataloging and reproduction. Except for correspondence, materials are organized *within* legajos by place of origin and then chronologically or alphabetically, according to the type of documentation (for example, for military service records). Correspondence was first organized by correspondent, then by place, and then chronologically within each correspondent's materials. Enclosures were kept with their covering letters, regardless of date, correspondent, and so forth. For filming, enclosures were placed immediately after the covering document to which they belonged. To maintain uniformity during the life of the project and among staff, O'Neill prepared a master table of organizational criteria embracing all types of documents found in the project and a standardized list of place-names with known variants.[6]

At the time that this methodology was agreed upon, no study had been done to see how it fit, if at all, with what little was known about the way that the materials had been organized when shipped from Havana, or—less certainly—New Orleans. Given the great disorder of the papers in most legajos both in 1912–15, when Roscoe R. Hill first examined them, and in 1976, when the project began, any attempt to recreate one or the other of these supposed "original" orders would have been fraught with difficulties.[7] More important, an attempt to recreate the supposed Havana organization of the papers would not have been consistent with the current practices of the Archive of the Indies.

As it turned out, the method used for correspondence was consistent with the vestiges of legajo organization that Roscoe Hill found when he worked on his catalog, at least for some legajos containing outbound correspondence from the governor's office before 1790. Legajos of inbound correspondence from the same office and dating before 1790 seem to have been organized by months. Legajos for the post-1790 period contained incoming and outgoing correspondence and a host of materials not immediately related to the letters, all indiscriminately mixed in no clear order.[8] No archivist would accept as an "archival order" worthy of preservation the sorts of disorder Hill recorded, although certain critics of the Cuban Papers Project apparently told NEH that it should be preserved.

Where legajos had been organized in recent times (as shown by penciled folio numbers), that organization, however defective, was respected. For example, legajos 1–59 had been organized in the 1950s along strictly chronological lines, even to the point of separating enclosures from their covering letters![9]

Once the materials in each legajo had been placed in an archivally acceptable order, each folio was numbered in pencil.[10] A typewritten table of contents was then prepared showing the major divisions of the legajo. The early tables of contents do not give inclusive folio numbers for these sections or any subsections, but the contents prepared after 1978 do. The table of contents is filmed at the beginning of each legajo's roll(s).

Relationship with NEH

It would be pleasant to be able to say that the Cuban Papers Project's relationship with NEH was amiable from beginning to end, but such was not the case. Staffing problems at Seville caused O'Neill to seek and obtain an extension on the project's three-year life during its second year, an extension he understood to allow the use of the funds until the entire 72 (half-time) person months originally budgeted had been expended. As it happened, NEH tightened up its rules for extensions at exactly the time that the original grant expired (September 30, 1980). Under the new rules, extensions were for one year at most and had to be justified in detail and be for explicitly defined purposes (plan of work), other than just spending the money in the budget.

When, therefore, O'Neill wanted to continue the project past September 30, 1981 (the end of the first extension, as defined by NEH's new rules), NEH demanded explanations and documentation. Because of certain complaints that it had received, NEH was especially interested in obtaining a detailed methodological justification for the project as a whole as a condition for a further extension.[11] For a variety of reasons, Dr. O'Neill declined to provide the materials in question. In the end, the author did and NEH granted a final extension until September 1982. After one further complication arising from unclear wording in the original grant proposal concerning who would pay for the LSU copy of the films produced under the grant, the NEH grant came to an end.[12]

Subsequent History

Conclusion of the NEH grant did not, however, conclude the project. With funds from LSU and, later, the Historic New Orleans Collection, the work of preparing the documents for microfilming continued into 1986. A decade was required to complete a project whose major portion seemed at first to be do-able in three years![13]

Production of the final microfilms is under way. In common with other similar projects, the Cuban Paper Project (LSU and the Historical New Orleans Collection are joint sponsors of the microfilming) is paying for positive copies from a master negative that is prepared and paid for by the Centro Nacional de Microfilm of Spain. Because the number of projects both at the AGI and elsewhere in Spain is great and the centro's staff is small, delays in production are inevitable. Two of the seven parts of the film (340 whole and partial reels) were produced during the NEH grant period. In January 1990, the master negative microfilm for the last of the seven parts of the project was finished at the AGI. Positive copies may be obtained from the Servicio Nacional de Microfilm, Madrid.

Conclusion

Four observations may be made by way of conclusion. First some materials, especially those dealing with West Florida after 1803, have yet to be prepared and filmed. The University of Florida, in cooperation with the Archive of the Indies and the Centro Nacional de Microfilm, has produced an edition of the West Florida treasury records, AGI, PC 228–82, except for the records of the hospitals and storehouses in the province. Thus the principal run of unfilmed materials is the one found in the papers of the captains-general of Cuba (except as noted here). Once prepared and filmed, these latter materials, together with the Santo Domingo Project and Cuban Papers Project materials, will give scholars access to at least 75 percent of the Spanish materials needed to study the Hispanic presence in the Mississippi Valley and along the Gulf Coast after 1763; that is, if diplomatic history is not considered.

A second observation is that if NEH funds projects involving further microfilming in Spanish archives, it will be helpful to all concerned if NEH obtains the services of a program specialist familiar with those archives and conditions in them. Even with the greatest goodwill and the most detailed, carefully worded methodological statements and plans of work at hand, no one who has not worked there can really understand why delays develop that cannot be ended as they might in the United States, or be able to judge the merits of complaints of seemingly equally qualified professionals about one another's work.

Third, the endowment should recognize as a matter of policy that it may have to relax strict enforcement of chronological limits on expenditures of grant funds in these cases. Our Spanish co-workers do the best that they can, and often more than we have any right to expect, but they cannot always do it to our timetables. Madrid's assistance can, of course, be obtained, but it is better in the long run to work within the given rules and institutions rather than invoke exceptions dictated from Madrid. NEH has to be sensitive to these matters if frustrations are to be minimized in connection with Quincentennial projects.

Finally, collection strategy is an important, if often unstated, ingredient in shaping the goals of a microfilming project. The Cuban Papers Project was intended to provide scholars with reproductions of materials in the Archive of the Indies that could be used in lieu of the originals, but cited as if the researcher were using the originals.[14] Institutionally, this would mean that a student or researcher could begin work in the United States confident that his/her citations of the documents would be the same as those produced by researchers in Seville, thus preserving scholarly communication while reducing the need for costly travel and the possibility of damage to the original paper through frequent handling. A further objective was to provide basic, but not exhaustively comprehensive, materials for teaching use on campus, a goal furthered by the fact that most Louisiana materials in the Archive of the Indies are found in three blocks (two in Papeles de Cuba, one in Santo Domingo).[15]

NEH might well wish to require statements of collection strategy from proponents of new microfilming and optical disk projects, the better to judge whether the resource to be created will serve a broad community by providing a basic core of materials that exactly duplicates the originals (which must be in an appropriate, more or less permanent archival order), or will build to a specialized collection that may not be widely useful because it is narrowly defined or uses forms of citation that do not match those of the originals.

NOTES

1. "Archivist's Preface" and "Technical Preface," in José de la Peña, *Catálogo de documentos del Archivo General de Indias, Sección V, Gobierno, Audiencia de Santo Domingo, Sobre la época Española de Lusiana*, 2 vols. (Madrid and New Orleans, 1968), pp. xxi–xxii, xxxv–xxxviii, respectively, and Charles E. O'Neill, "Recollections of the Archivo General de Indias," in *El Archivo en Mi Recuerdo* (Seville, 1986), p. 121.

2. O'Neill intended to pay his workers a monthly salary, which would have made them state employees had LSU contributed to those salaries, and thus raised a host of insoluble legal problems. Instead, we planned to pay Loyola a "service charge" for each reel of film supplied under the project. Subsequently, when LSU assumed the responsibility for paying for the preparation of the legajos, we paid on a piece rate, for "professional services," and thus avoided the problems that a salary would have raised.

3. Ibid., p. 126.

4. These form a discontinuous series, of which legajos 1137, 1145–47, 1232–33, 1394, 1425, and 1440–44 cover the years 1771–96. The series continues in legajos 1446, 1447, 1500–02, 1550–56, and 1572–74. Other omissions were correspondence with officials at Natchez, legajos 2351–56, and correspondence with James Wilkinson, legajos 2373–75.

5. This is a larger total than the number of legajos. Some numbers have A, B, and even C parts, each a legajo by itself.

6. Charles E. O'Neill, "Criterios y Reglas Generales," and untitled lists of places in Louisiana and Florida Occidental, typescript, n.d., n.p., collection of the author.

7. Hill identified at least 252 legajos as "disordered" and said that "if the disordered legajos could ever be put in order, it would, of course, be a great improvement": Roscoe R. Hill, *Descriptive Catalogue of the Documents relating to the History of the United States in the Papeles Procedentes de Cuba* (Washington, DC: 1916), p. xxvii.

8. For the organization Hill found, see his descriptions for legajos 1–188; Paul E. Hoffman to Dr. Margaret Childs (NEH), January 27, 1982, collection of the author, is a lengthy analysis of this problem.

9. One of the project's staff spent 160 hours on one of these legajos, carefully reuniting letters and their enclosures. Because of a prior decision by the archive not to undo organizational work previously done, however defective from many points of view, and the amount of time required, which made similar reorganization of the remaining 58 legajos uneconomic given the time and financial restraints of the project, this legajo had to be put back into its strictly chronological order. The incident illustrates the importance of placing materials into the best possible organization before numbering and filming; once filmed, the archive is reluctant to change the order of documents because of concerns that this might disrupt scholarly citation.

10. The Santo Domingo Project used a mechanical stamping machine.

11. These complaints came from another NEH-supported project that was creating a calendar of unique noncirculating holdings and accordingly had a different microfilming strategy that required only that folio numbers be placed on the documents before filming (for ease in locating them on microfilm reels), regardless of their organization within the legajos. Because some of the legajos of interest to that project fell within the scope of the Cuban Papers Project, that project felt itself in conflict with us over this methodological point and made ill-informed charges about our methodology. In fact, the other project was

in conflict with the AGI's standing policies governing the microfilming of entire legajos, not with some arbitrary rules devised by the Cuban Papers Project.

12. NEH agreed to pay for the second copy of the film from unexpended grant funds since the language of the proposal could be understood in that fashion and monies had been expended for two copies when the first part of the film was duplicated.

13. Allowing for periods when fewer than two people were employed or when there were interruptions in the work, but factoring in work done by the University of Southwestern Louisiana on legajos 188–221, the project took about nine years' work by a part-time staff of two.

14. It is particularly important that U.S. institutions holding photocopies of AGI materials with the pre-1929 legajo numbers develop and append to their collections a table giving the post-1929 legajo numbers. To do otherwise is to condemn their modern users to speak in a language of citation unintelligible to other scholars.

15. Exhaustive, comprehensive collections seemed an unrealistic goal since each historian defines the limits of his/her research in unique ways once certain central (or basic) bodies or records have been used.

12. *"Ain't No Road to Candelaria"*

The New World Archives—A Dream in the Desert

Until today I never thought about the New World archives in west Texas terms. Nearly two years ago Tom Naylor, my agnostic trail companion—who has stuck by me with more faith than I have often placed in God—and I were in the west Texas desert searching out an old presidio site. Following the best of modern topographic maps, we rumbled into a cluster of ranch buildings to ask directions to Candelaria. The door to the ranch house opened, and a strapping Texan in his late twenties strode toward our Blazer.

"Howdy."

"Hi. We're looking for the road to Candelaria."

"Candelaria."

"Yep. We think it should be that road," pointing to an obvious cut into a hill about a mile off.

"Ain't no road to Candelaria."

"But if you look at this U.S. topo map, it . . ."

"Ain't no road to Candelaria. Wher' you'n fr'm?"

"Arizona. We're doing historical research for the National Archives and need to get to Candelaria."

"Huggh. Ain't no road to Candelaria." The screen door creaked open about a foot. "Daddy, these here guys want to go to Candelaria. I tol'em they ain't no road to Candalaria. Ain't no road, is there, Daddy?"

The door widened. A muscular farmer in his sixties, clad in overalls, stared us down. "Ain't no road to Candelaria."

We were about to insist by appealing to reason, science, observation, and western hospitality. That's when we saw Daddy's middle son cradling a long-barreled Winchester in his burly arms, backing up Daddy's verdict and his brother's veracity. Obviously, they were quite right: there was no road to Candelaria—at least not from the U.S. Post Office.

"You'ns jes' take that well travelled road strait east—hear?"

We certainly did. We heard the words, and the clicks. There's one thing about west Texas—their lessons on proprietorship are Cartesian: clear and distinct. We got the idea.

My west Texas story has much to do with the New World Archives—not the least of which is how to get there from here, together with traditional notions about proprietorship. Maybe there "ain't no road to Candelaria," but sure as hell, there is a Candelaria.

New Year's morning 1983 was crisp and clear blue. As I awoke to the late dawn light, my brain engaged and I found myself saying, "That's it! The New World Archives." Days of muddled thinking had converged. Now whether that was a historic moment of conception or contraception, only time will tell.

The New World Archives, I thought, would be an international, non-profit organization, funded by participating nation-states and philanthropic foundations, directed by a small staff under the guidance of a board of archival and end-user directors. The New World Archive itself would not become a depository, that is, an archive in the traditional sense of the word; rather, it would attempt to gather reproductions of New World–related documents, making them accessible throughout the Americas, especially by providing more elaborate finding aids. The collective power of the New World Archive was not to be focused on the whole array of archival problems associated with building architecture, humidity control, or document conservation. The concept of the New World Archive was based on the premise that the ultimate reason for document conservation is information preservation, and that information preserved by reproduction also had to provide some ready access. Another aspect of the project was to have been the establishment of a program of priorities whereby the financial potentials of the organization could assist in the rapid reproductive preservation of those documents most in danger of disintegration. One of the practical issues raised by this program was precisely the identification of already reproduced documents, which is the central concern of this conference—although for slightly different reasons.

The idea of the New World Archive is based on the reality that the written record of the cultural past of the Americas resides mainly in non-American nations. From native to immigrant we are bereft of our earliest patrimony without major cooperative commitments from such nations. Today there is no New World Archive. There are bits and tatters here and there; some bits are big, and some tatters are fairly well stitched together. But the body of evidence is neither well known nor well consulted.

For years, like most of you, I have enjoyed the beneficent services of Spanish, Italian, and Latin American archives. For years, like most of you, I rooted in these precious treasures with not a little suppressed guilt and growing concern because I knew that every request I penciled would send a blue-coated archive porter out to bring back a string-bound legajo to my desk. How long can these papers endure the onslaught of scholarly ignorance? And did my investigative goals justify the deterioration of evidence that would be required by an as-yet unborn scholar greater than I?

I work at the land-grant university in a sparsely populated state. There has been neither money nor interest enough to acquire even a fourth-class archival collection. And even if there were enough financial resources, there is not much around that is not already owned. Yet, as responsible, creative historians, we still have a need to know about our total past in perspectives that are pertinent to our experiences and social needs. Our professional plight is nearly the same as the plight of the New World's native peoples—our history lies locked in the Archives of Elsewhere.

When I visited those archives of elsewhere—be it Bancroft, Beineke, Benson, Brown, or the Indies, I suffered the same agony: How could I find what I sought within the limits of time and money? My reaction was uncommon because I then set out to create a computerized finding aid for our region's history and anthropology. This was a guide to primary materials beyond the scope of the customary calendar or catalog, which unfortunately have the practical effect of sending one leafing through stacks of papers—seeing what scores have seen before—to ferret out one's own flavorful nut. If the desert was too poor to own the treasures of its history, perhaps a computer map to the treasures of elsewhere would be the next best thing.

My approach, and by extension, that of the New World Archive, has unintentionally offended librarians, confounded archivists, and roiled the calm waters of traditional scholarship. Nevertheless, I knew that we held no hope of ever possessing the physical documents—the pieces of primary evidence—of our past; we could never placidly reside in our desert and explain ourselves without far more detailed information than provided by catalogs.

As for funding in general, may I confess that I too have savored the sweet and sour of the National Endowment for the Humanities. In fairness to the agency, however, I know my approaches have rankled the panels of my peers more than our public servants. We all know our basic financial needs far exceed the paltry sums doled out to the nonuniformed transients in academe. As I have lamented before, I read regularly of military jets crashing on training missions in the desert—any of which would fund our archival needs for a decade! I dare to draw these odious comparisons because I truly believe that our societal priorities are misplaced. I believe the fullest grasp of the cultural interfacing of the American, that is, the New World, experience is absolutely essential for the next phase of human expansion—if it is to be positive and progressive. To lose the past is to lose the future. Not only are we subject to making the same mistakes, we cannot identify the pillars of progress upon which to build. West Texas may well be barren precisely because there ain't no road to Candelaria.

Much of what has been discovered or may yet be discovered about the cultures of the Americas lies in archival collections of non-American nations. We cannot ask those nations to relinquish their patrimony, and yet their control of our patrimony is so absolute that we in the Americas will always stand in jeopardy of losing the evidence of our histories. More than that, the record of discovery and culture change throughout the world since the Columbian voyages is the greatest single body of knowledge about directed culture change in the history of mankind. Neither the world nor man in it will ever again be where he was five hundred years ago. We cannot allow that record to be lost. We cannot allow that record to be diminished any more. We cannot afford to limit access to this complex evidence that can help us build roads to new understandings. And this does not pertain only to the imperial archives of Europe; it pertains to provincial archives in the Americas.

We have already heard reference to frustrations and budget blocking. We know that scholarship depends not only on a wealth of information but on wealth itself for the acquisition, maintenance, and access to that information. You may not share my outspoken view if you hail from mahogany or oak studies whose hallowed collections are down the hall or across the yard. I still see myself beside the saguaro in my colonial desert from which the silver and gold was extracted to enrich the collections of distant baronies. Am I any different from the native American, the immigrant criollo, or the scholar of tomorrow? Where do we go when the words of past realities are gone from our desert?

These words are not written in anger. They simply describe the situation—however, they do plead for alternatives. Like the New World Archive, they raise the question of the economics of information, which leads to one of the most basic issues of the human condition: the ethics of knowledge, the right to know, and the duty to inform, to educate. We chant that the truth shall make us free, but knowledge must precede truth if truth is knowledge that conforms to reality. Ignorance is slavery under the tyranny of not knowing. To what degree can any of us in the information chain subject our knowledge to the pure principles of private ownership? This question usually remains unasked because almost instinctively we know that knowledge is power, and power is something we rarely share lest it be turned against us. Herein lies the dilemma of the New World Archives!

Our historical world is divided into two classes: the providers and the users. Archivists are given what others wish saved, the rest is shredded. So the primary task of the archivist is salvation (of paper). Historians are the demon users who breathe chaos into institutional order and destroy the fragile record by our insistence to shuffle it again and again in search of evidence. The miracle of microfilm reduced some of this wear and tear while preserving the chaos already introduced into the organization of the record. When users, like myself, suggested systematic microfilming, archivists scoffed. Even if we did succeed in filming entire archives, there was no guarantee that the film would outlast the documents—and duplication of the reproductions was inexorably subject to qualitative degradation. The archivists' arguments carried the day.

When I introduced the idea of the New World Archives during a private conference at the Archivo General de Indias in 1984, I played the role of Don Quixote chasing an impossible dream. Not even realizing the aversion to microfilm, I blithely preached the gospel of high technology, but there was no Constantine to hear my words. However, I have come to think that one or another of those dear lady archivists in attendance was a Santa Elena. Just this last fall, the Ministry of Culture, the Ramón Areces Foundation, and IBM of Spain announced their intentions to bring high technology to the Archive of the Indies. It is possible that a new road is being built to Candelaria?

If a New World Archive is ever to exist, its genes will have to be binary because this is the only structure that will supersede any species of information storage or retrieval. By this I mean, there is no more basic codification of data than 0/1, plus or minus, go or no-go, or in Shakespearean terms, "to be or not to be." This is no longer the question; it is the answer. The total capability to capture complete graphic images of documents is highly advanced; the capability of duplication and dissemination without degradation is a fundamental characteristic of this technology; and the preservation of original information without distortion and deception is achievable.

Digital technology has bent the barrel of the archivist's long rifle. There is a road to Candelaria, and we are on it. Someone can and may rearm the middle son of ignorance. The future may remain as barren as west Texas. But somehow I don't think so.

In the past two and half years since I knew I would serve, and indeed, have served on the U.S. Columbus Jubilee Quincentenary Commission, I have learned a great deal about things I have taken for granted. Rethinking the discovery of the Americas has led to an encounter with myself and more genuine appraisals of community. Most of us are teachers, and I am sure you will agree that arrays of ideas are best understood when the umbrella concept under which they are presented is clearly defined. This is but another way of saying that our concepts must be big enough to contain our perceptions. This is precisely what I see as capable of happening during this celebration. Like Columbus we are thrust full body against the wall of ignorance created by human arrogance and intellectual timidity. Efficient access to total information will force us to think, and think maturely. If we, and I speak of us as a cultural species of mankind, if we are to meet the challenge of the information revolution, we must learn to put aside our adolescent fictions from plagiarism to fantasy and revel in the complex world of adult relationships. If we do not, other people will. And those people will hold the power of the future. For myself, I can see no better inaugural contribution to the coming millennium than launching the New World Archives as a model of information preservation and exchange. Among the things I have learned on the Columbus commission is that it is better to speak of the Americas than America, and that the discovery of the New World is not just in contrast to the Old—because 1492 was the moment Spaceship Earth first realized its architecture. It was then that Earth became the world in the mind of man, and that was new.

We live in momentous times. Although we talk of old paper and preservation, we talk of revolution in the way we share and process our knowledge. Are we strong enough to face the challenge? Are we generous enough to share the pride and pratfalls of the past? Are we shrewd enough to realize that our place in history may just be to put history in its place? Are we wise enough to restrict our competitiveness to issues of quality and not proprietorship? These are hard issues. They are human issues. Well answered, these are the new roads to Candelaria. Unanswered, the flame of Candelaria will flicker like a dying sun, and our bones will bleach in the cold deserts of our own making.

DOUGLAS E. JONES

13. *Alabama and the De Soto Expedition*

A Case Study in Archival Opportunity

During its five-year existence (1985–90), the Alabama De Soto Commission undertook a number of historical and archaeological investigations in an effort to reconstruct the travel route of the Hernando de Soto expedition through the state in 1540. Soto was the first European to penetrate the interior of La Florida—a territory that included what is now Alabama and most of the southeastern United States. The commission's diverse membership included Soto scholars and others knowledgeable of aboriginal sites in the region.

Created by an executive order of the governor to commemorate the 450th anniversary of the event, the Alabama De Soto Commission was to direct research related to sixteenth-century Spanish exploration and colonization in Alabama, designate sections of existing highways as the De Soto Trail, and plan public events relating to Soto's travels in the state. The commission also was charged with identifying sites having potential for development into cultural and historic attractions and with publicizing its findings through a variety of media. Finally, there existed a strong commitment to enhance public awareness about the importance of early European contacts to the history and cultural traditions of the state.

The reasons for creating this commission were several. Alabama has a long and impressive Indian heritage known primarily through a wealth of archaeological materials collected across the state and region, mostly during the last fifty years. The majority of these collections reside in the State Museum of Natural History, a division of the University of Alabama. The museum's computerized archaeological site file numbers more than 8,000 records, of which nearly 6,000 are from Alabama and several contiguous states.

The Moundville archaeological site, a unit of the Alabama State Museum and the largest and best preserved Mississippian Indian cultural center in the United States, may have been on Soto's route to Mississippi following the devastating battle at the Indian village of Mabila in late 1540.

A second basis for undertaking this study is the generally accepted premise that Soto's route through Alabama was extensive, and that he followed Indian trails connecting a number of major population centers whose archaeological records likely are in the state site file. The great battle between Soto and the Choctaw chief Tuscaluza at Mabila, according to all the historical records, took place somewhere in Alabama. Finally, our involvement in this venture would be an appropriate contribution to the Columbus Quincentenary and to the people of Alabama, whose understanding and appreciation of Spanish influence on their heritage are based on scant treatment in school textbooks and public media.

The degree of public interest this work has created in Alabama and elsewhere in the Southeast has been gratifying. It is obvious that tales of explorers, hardships, and great battles continue to trigger the imagination of the public. The 150–year gap in our history, from Soto's departure in 1540 until the arrival of the French in the early 1700s, also is of interest to a number of individuals associated with the Alabama De Soto Commission.

In light of Alabama's large and significant archaeological collections, including a number of sixteenth-century Spanish artifacts, initial efforts focused on the physical evidence of the De Soto expeditions, an aspect of investigation that received little attention by Chairman John Swanton and the U.S. De Soto Expedition Commission fifty years ago. Indeed, current archaeological sophistication in regard to the Southeast began to develop only in the 1950s. Unless one could correlate historic accounts with archaeological evidence, no real conclusions could be reached. Consequently, field excavations of possible Mabila battle sites were undertaken.

The justification to search for a site that had been sought unsuccessfully for over 400 years was that Mabila's archaeological profile should be distinctive from that of any other site in Alabama or, indeed, the entire Southeast. Although a relatively new and small tributary site, Mabila was the locale of a battle pitting more than 600 Spanish soldiers against unknown thousands of Indians. One should expect to find there bits of chain mail, crossbow bolt tips, broken and discarded equipment, and other battlefield debris. The site may contain Spanish graves and remains of some of the several thousand Indian casualties. According to all known chronicles of the expedition, the fortified town was burned during the battle. No other Indian site in Alabama should exhibit these particular characteristics.

The discovery of Mabila—the most significant point on Soto's route in Alabama—would enhance the possibility of locating other towns encountered by the Spanish before and after the event. At Mabila it became obvious to Soto's officers and men that the expedition was doomed, but the governor pushed on, driven by ambition and the fear of failure, only to die two years later along the Mississippi River.

Despite the wealth of archaeological materials found in the past fifty years, no site in Alabama, and few elsewhere in the region, have yielded unequivocal physical evidence of De Soto's presence. Many sixteenth-century Spanish artifacts have been found in the state, mostly by amateurs, but we cannot distinguish with certainty between Soto items and those of later expeditions, especially that of Tristán de Luna in 1559–61. The question of Mabila's location and Soto's travel through the state will remain unanswered until specifics are known about the trade goods, armor, weapons, and equipment that Soto brought into La Florida. This lack of documentary evidence regarding the outfitting of the expedition is a major deterrent to route reconstructions.

The principal focus of investigative attention to Soto's travels in the Southeast remains an archival one, principally the writing of individuals who were participants in the enterprise. Although these chronicles likely are familiar to most readers, a brief recapitulation may be useful.

The account favored most by modern scholars seems to be that of an unknown "Gentleman of Elvas" entitled "True Relation of the Hardships Suffered by Governor Fernando De Soto and Certain Portuguese Gentlemen During the Discovery of the Province of Florida." Written in Portuguese in 1557, four years after the return of the expedition's survivors, this was the first of the Soto narratives. Translated frequently over the years into Dutch, French, and English, the 1926 version by James A. Robertson seems to be the most popular modern English text. This is an elegant two-volume facsimile of the original Portuguese with a translation, copious notes, and bibliographic references done under the aegis of the Florida State Historical Society.

The account by Garcilaso de la Vega ("The Inca"), apparently completed in 1591, is based primarily on the recollections of Gonzalo Silvestre, a minor figure with the expedition. The longest of the four Soto chronicles, Garcilaso's work is highly romanticized, making the governor a hero in the eyes of readers. Some experts consider this version unreliable regarding details.

The writing of Luis Hernandez de Biedma comprises the third major source for Soto studies. The shortest of the accounts, Biedma's relation, according to James Robertson, "bears more or less the stamp of an official report on the expedition, and did, in fact, find its way into the Spanish archives or offices as early as 1544."[1] Along with Garcilaso's report, this is considered by some experts to be of little use in locating the activities of Soto and his men.

The last of the standard works is that of Rodrigo Ranjel, De Soto's private secretary. The original manuscript has not been located, but apparently much of its substance is preserved in a manuscript by Gonzalo Fernández de Oviedo published in Madrid in 1851 and included in translations by Robertson and Bourne. The U.S. De Soto Commission considered Ranjel's treatment superior even to that of Elvas in understanding the sequence of events and placing of the route "so far as it goes."[2] Surviving parts of the original manuscript, as incorporated by Oviedo, cover the route from the landing in Florida in 1539 to the winter campsite in Mississippi in 1541.

The chronicles of post–De Soto expeditions have been useful to some investigators. DePratter, Hudson, and Smith have found the accounts of the Juan Pardo expedition of 1566–67 from the South Carolina coast particularly important in corroborating observations of the four narratives enumerated above. They conclude that Juan Pardo's route included five towns visited by Soto twenty years earlier. The accounts of Tristán de Luna's abortive efforts in 1559–61 to establish the first Spanish colony La Florida in the area of Pensacola Bay are also valuable to Soto researchers. Luna had great difficulty finding towns visited by Soto in spite of the fact that some survivors of the earlier expedition were members of his company. Four hundred and fifty years after the event, scholars suffer the same frustration experienced by Luna only twenty years after.

The Alabama De Soto Commission considered several De Soto route "hypotheses" (some experts dislike this term because it implies the ultimate possibility of proof, which some think is unlikely). "Proof" in the final analysis may be limited to the presence or absence of two Spanish trade items thought to have been associated exclusively with the Soto expedition: small multicolored Nueva Cádiz beads and sheet brass Clarksdale bells. Both were found in mid-sixteenth-century archaeological contexts in South America. Discovered mostly as grave goods at a number of late Mississippian archaeological sites in the Southeast, these may be the only physical evidence of Soto's passing. Whether carried by Indians far from the army's route, or lost, discarded, or cached along the route itself, these artifacts and their distribution must be related in some manner to the actual path of Soto. The relationship among beads, bells, and mid-sixteenth century Indian sites in Alabama must be important. Therefore, the Alabama commission's investigations took several new directions.

Having failed to locate Mabila or any other key site, the Alabama group developed a synthesis of what is known today about Indian occupations in Alabama in 1540, based on existing archaeological data. A number of large artifact collections gathered from sites in the valleys of the Coosa and Alabama rivers over the past fifty years were reevaluated in light of the route hypotheses under consideration. A computer with multilayering data capacity was used to make a complete map of all known late Mississippian Indian sites and Spanish artifacts for Alabama and several other states in the Southeast. On this base could be superimposed topography, streams, landforms, and general geology and soil types to determine if there is a pattern to the distribution of protohistoric occupations and Spanish materials. It may be possible to establish a corridor along which Soto is likely to have traveled; selected excavations within this corridor ultimately may prove to be productive.

None of the four standard chronicles provides sufficient details regarding directions and distances traveled, terrain crossed, or Indian cultures encountered to reconstruct Soto's travel route. One must remember that Soto was here for God, gold, and glory, not to conduct a careful geographic or ethnographic survey of the region. Unless new historic accounts of the expedition are found and can be related to specific archaeological sites and known geographic features, the route followed by this group of Spanish through the Southeast will remain a mystery. Here are a few possibilities that may be relevant for Soto studies:

1. Documentation should exist relating to Soto's Cuba-based reconnaissance of the Florida coast prior to his landing in the summer of 1539; letters to his wife in Cuba may contain pertinent comments on the area.

2. Garcilaso de la Vega's detailed description of the region between Tampa and Tallahassee implies that he had access to earlier reports (perhaps those of Cabeza de Vaca).

3. Cargo manifests of ships bringing De Soto's army to Florida would be of critical importance in reconstructing an inventory of trade goods, supplies, and equipment carried by the expedition.

4. There must be other accounts of expedition participants somewhere in the Spanish archives. Surely, the four known documents do not represent the total treatment of an event of this significance, even though it was a complete failure in the eyes of Soto's contemporaries.

5. Other maps of the northern coast of the Gulf of Mexico must exist. The Spanish appear to have made a number of forays along the coast, all the way from Cuba to the western gulf.

6. Documents clarifying the distance measure employed by Soto will be important in reconstructing the distribution of towns and events along the route. The Swanton Commission concluded that the *legua legal* (2.63 miles) was the proper unit. The longer *legua comun* (3.45) is preferred by some modern scholars. Men who could accurately determine latitudes in the New World certainly could accurately chart coastlines, map harbors, and calculate distances traveled on land. It is difficult to believe that these geographic references were no more than rough estimates, as some think today.

Based on the preponderance of evidence considered by the Alabama De Soto Commission, the Alabama Highway Route of the De Soto Trail has been established and appropriate marker signs placed at ten-mile intervals throughout its 350-mile length. Kiosk exhibits and brochures describing the expedition have been placed at highway visitor centers and key geographic points, as indeterminate as they may be at this time. A mobile Soto exhibit now is touring Alabama, with particular attention given to public schools. Although the official investigations of the Alabama De Soto Commission are completed, attempts by professionals and lay people to track Soto and his army through Alabama will continue.

Efforts persist on a national level to establish a new federal Soto commission, the dream of Florida senator Bob Graham, to encourage and coordinate research throughout the Southeast and, it is hoped, to mount a major archival search in the United States and in Europe.

In spite of serious disagreements among experts regarding the Soto travel route in the New World, much serious work has been undertaken and the imagination of the public has been captured during this 450th anniversary period. During its existence, the Alabama De Soto Commission published and distributed to hundreds of scholars, lay people, and the general public thirteen issues of "The De Soto Working Papers" reporting on work in Alabama and elsewhere in the Southeast. New archival data and continued archaeological investigations are essential to our clearer understanding of this important historic event.

In 1981 the University of Alabama convened a symposium entitled "Alabama and the Borderlands." A paper on European penetrations in eastern North America read by the late John Parry of Harvard included a fitting closure for this report of De Soto in Alabama.

> Asia-in-the-West, that seductive mirage, had no place in his plans or his instructions-nor, indeed, had geographic inquiry of any kind, except for the 200 leagues of the Gulf Coast that he was to explore and on which he was told to found three towns (but did not). His achievement must be judged in relation to what he undertook. By that criterion the expedition-so well prepared, so ill conducted-was a failure. He found no treasure, except a box of inferior freshwater pearls, because there was none to find. More significantly, it struck no roots, left no serious trace. Modern scholars cannot agree on even the exact route of his aimless, wandering army.
>
> Soto's aimlessness was a subject of severe comment by all the contemporary chroniclers. "He went about for five years hunting mines," wrote López de Gomara, "thinking it would be like Peru. He made no settlement, and thus he died, and destroyed those who went with him. Never will conquerors do well unless they settle before they undertake anything else, especially here where the Indians are valiant bowmen and strong." Soto's failure, no doubt, is among the reasons why this symposium is conducted today in English, not Spanish.[3]

NOTES

1. John R. Swanton, Final Report of the United States De Soto Expedition Commission, 76th Congress, 1st session, House Document 71 (Washington, DC: GPO, 1939), p. 6.
2. Ibid., p. 9.
3. John H. Parry, "European Penetrations of Eastern North America," in *Alabama and the Borderlands: From Prehistory to Statehood* (Tuscaloosa, AL: University of Alabama Press, 1985), pp. 94–95.

BIBLIOGRAPHY

Badger, R. R., and Clayton, L. A., eds. *Alabama and the Borderlands: From Prehistory to Statehood.* Tuscaloosa: University of Alabama Press, 1985.

Biedma, Luís Hernández de. "Relation of the Conquest of Florida." In *Narratives of the Career of Hernando de Soto in the Conquest of Florida,* ed. Edward G. Bourne. New York: A. S. Barnes, 1904.

DePratter, C. B., Hudson, C. M., and Smith, M. T. "The Route of Juan Pardo's Explorations in the Interior Southeast, 1566–68." *Florida Historical Quarterly* 62 (October 1983):125–58.

Parry, John H. "European Penetration of Eastern North America." In *Alabama and the Borderlands: From Prehistory to Statehood*. Tuscaloosa: University of Alabama Press, 1985.

Ranjel, Rodrigo. "A Narrative of De Soto's Expedition." In *Narratives of the Career of Hernando de Soto*, trans. Buckingham Smith, ed. Edward G. Bourne. New York: Allerton, 1922.

Robertson, James A., trans. *A Gentleman of Elvas, True Relation of the Hardship Suffered by Governor Fernando de Soto and Certain Portuguese Gentlemen During the Discovery of the Province of Florida*, 2 vols. DeLand, FL: Florida State Historical Society, 1932.

Swanton, John R. *Final Report of the United States De Soto Expedition Commission*. 76th Congress, 1st session, House Document 71. Washington, DC: GPO, 1939.

Vega, Garcilaso de la. *The Florida of the Inca*, ed. John G. Varner and Jeanette J. Varner. Austin: University of Texas Press, 1967.

MICHAEL C. SCARDAVILLE

14. The Southeastern Columbus Quincentennial Project

The Southeastern Columbus Quincentenary Commission represents a grass-roots initiative for the 1992 celebration. The newly formed commission is a regional consortium of ten states that, by pooling resources and talents, aims to maximize their ability to plan for the Quincentenary.

The following mission statement perhaps best defines the nature and purpose of the commission:

> The Southeastern Columbus Quincentenary Commission was organized in 1987 to develop, coordinate, and support regional programming associated with the 1992 Quincentenary. The goal is to ensure that the Southeast takes full advantage of the opportunity provided by the Quincentenary to enhance scholarly and public understanding of the region's diverse historical origins and cultural developments since 1492 in as effective and efficient manner possible. The result will be programming that reflects on the consequences, both historical and contemporary, of contact among the European, African, and Indian cultures both within the region and within the broader context of the Caribbean basin.
>
> The Commission to date includes representatives of state humanities councils, colleges and universities, museums, and other cultural organizations in the Southeast who believe that the region possesses common historical and cultural roots and shares contemporary concerns and issues resulting from the voyages of Columbus. The Commission members further believe that these commonalties should be the basis for regional programming and that the combining of resources of institutions and organizations in the region offers the most efficient and effective way to undertake the study and promote the awareness of how Columbus affected the development of the southeast during the past five centuries.

The state humanities councils took the initiative in the formation of the commission. In anticipation of interest in the Quincentenary, the councils, a component of the National Endowment for the Humanities, hoped to avoid funding numerous and possibly overlapping projects on a state-by-state basis. Several council directors recognized that state humanities monies could be more effectively used if programs cut across state lines and that any Columbus-related programming, by its very nature, should be done on a regional basis. Since the Spanish, Indians, and others did not think in contemporary political jurisdictions, a strong case could be made for viewing the Southeast as a cultural entity for the Quincentenary projects.

Under the auspices of the state humanities councils in the Southeast, planning meetings were held in Charleston, South Carolina, in December 1986 and in Atlanta, Georgia, in March 1987 to explore the potential for regional cooperation. The Atlanta meeting, funded by minigrants from each participating state council, was attended by twenty-five humanists representing universities, state historical societies, state museums, public television, the Columbus Quincentenary Commission, the National Endowment for the Humanities, Partners for Livable Places, and other organizations.

The Atlanta meeting proved successful in three ways. To explore regional programming possibilities, the participants identified several themes and issues as well as a number of complementary formats. Although the geographical limits were easily defined by broader historical and cultural patterns, no temporal limits were set in order to focus on the historical process over the past five hundred years. The participants identified three themes that would underscore this continuity: (1) the Columbian exchange, noting cultural contact and interplay among southeastern cultures; (2) adaptation and accommodation to the New World environment among cultural groups, stressing language, material culture, and attitudes toward one another; (3) the Southeast and the Caribbean, focusing on such topics as changing demographic patterns and competition for empire in the colonial and national periods. The discussants also suggested that these and other issues would be best presented through a variety of formats, including scholarship, museum exhibits (tied to conferences, if possible), public school packets, and audio and visual materials.

A second accomplishment of the Atlanta meeting was to identify possible monies and funding strategies. The participants discussed the most effective ways to package a variety of grant proposals. Having a representative present from NEH proved worthwhile in debating such strategies. It became evident, for instance, that grant proposals, given the structure of the endowment, had to be earmarked specifically for its various divisions.

A third accomplishment was the recognition of a need for an institutional base for the organization. The participants agreed that a secretariat was essential to avoid duplication of regional programs and to promote the development of joint projects and proposals. Moreover, the commission and its secretariat would constitute an official entity that would enable the participating groups in the Southeast to solicit funds for broadly based projects.

After advertising and receiving proposals over the summer, the states representing the commission awarded the secretariat to the University of Alabama in September 1987. In its multidisciplinary proposal, Alabama made an impressive commitment in terms of salaries, staff support, and expenses. With the selection of commission members, the structure of the Southeastern Columbus Quincentenary Commission is complete. What now awaits us is to implement those ideas discussed in Atlanta and to encourage other recommendations and projects.

In closing, I wish to suggest the possibility that the commission can serve as one of a number of groups that can offer broad support for a guide to Hispanic manuscripts in the United States. Support from such grass-roots organizations might very well enhance the funding possibilities and successful completion of the guide project.

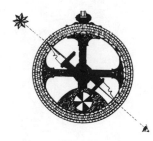

4 · Technology

Introduction to Part 4

The sometimes Byzantine world of the technological revolution is brought squarely into view by the chapter contributed by José Luis Becerril and his colleagues. It is a technical piece in the main, describing the bites and bytes of the Spanish project to copy over 7 million pages from the Archive of the Indies. It is the brave new world that John Kessell looks at with a somewhat jaundiced eye but one that is nonetheless here today and quite well might be the norm for the future.

JOSÉ LUIS BECERRIL
MIGUEL LATASA
MARGARITA VÁZQUEZ DE PARGA

15. The General Archive of the Indies Project

Introduction

Within the framework of activities to commemorate the Quincentennial of America's discovery, the Spanish Ministry of Culture, IBM Spain, and the Ramón Areces Foundation have signed a cooperative protocol to design and develop an information system for the General Archive of the Indies (AGI), the most important repository of documentation for the history of the discovery of the New World and of the Spanish administration of America. The project will last until the end of 1992.

This chapter begins with a brief description of the AGI and the general objectives of the project as background, while the rest is dedicated to explaining in more detail the architectural issues and technical aspects about the textual and image data bases.[1]

General Archive of the Indies

The AGI was founded in Seville two centuries ago by Charles III. The aim of this archive was to gather in a single site the Indies' documentation, which at that time was scattered throughout Spain, namely among Simancas, Cádiz, and Seville.

Thanks to the bureaucracy that left written records of every major decision taken between the sixteenth and nineteenth centuries, the documents held in Seville represent the detailed testimony of what the Spanish actuation was, over a huge territory in America (from the South of the United States to Tierra del Fuego) and the Philippines.

The archive is organized in fifteen sections according to the origin of the records. It contains 43,175 bundles. If we assume an average of 1,000 folios per bundle, many of them written on both sides, we estimate around 82 million pages of manuscript texts in the whole archive. Additionally, the section of Maps and Drawings holds about 7,000 pieces.

Appendix A contains two examples of documents, a letter and a halftone version of a map.

In addition to the original manuscript documents, there is a set of inventories, catalogs, and indexes containing all the description tools created by the archivists during the archive's lifetime. These description tools contain information for locating documents, abstracts of their contents, and other items.

In summary, there are two types of information in the AGI: visual, such as manuscript documents, maps, and drawings; and textual, such as description tools.

In 1986, a total of 17,037 researchers visited the archive, requesting more than 73,000 documents and 5,000 maps for examination. The demand for microfilm and photocopies was about 500,000 during that year.

Project Objectives

The general objectives of the project are:

1. Social: To preserve the historical heritage and at the same time increase its security and access capabilities.

2. Scientific: To develop an information system for historical archives.

3. Technological: To investigate the adaption of computer-based techniques (such as data bases, image processing, and local area networks) to document manipulation.

4. Specific: To contribute in a significant way to the commemoration activities of the Quincentenary of the discovery of America (1992).

These objectives will develop an information system that will be installed and operational in the AGI with the following main functions:

1. To provide researchers with a way to the information and documents of the archive by means of a Textual Data Base with all the description tools mentioned above.

2. To allow visualization of previously digitized documents in high-quality

image terminals, sparing thus the original ones from being handled. These digitized documents will be held in an Image Data File, from which they will be distributed to the users.

3. To automate administration matters of the archive, in particular those related to researchers' work (research statistics, movements of documents, and so forth).

In summary, the system will contain, as textual information, the whole set of existing inventories, catalogs and indexes and, as visual information, all the existing maps and drawings, plus about 9 million pages (11 percent of the archive) by 1992. This digitized information (the copied documents) should serve approximately 40 percent of those normally viewed annually. Important benefits for the conservation of the original documents will be obtained since, once digitized, hand manipulation will decrease.

The fact searching, the direct display on screen, and the facility to obtain copies at the touch of a key will dramatically enhance the use of the records by researchers and archivists.

Architectural Issues

System Requirements

In order to facilitate the implementation of the system in other archives, to reduce major software and hardware changes, and because of the different types of information involved, the system has to meet the following requirements:

1. Flexibility, to allow for modifications occurring in technology during the life cycle that will not affect the overall structure of the system.
2. Modularity, to allow the inclusion of new functions and/or the merging of several functions into a new one.
3. Clear interfaces with the specialized devices to allow upgrading without modifications.
4. Portability of all the developed applications.

System Architecture

The best answer to the system requirements is an architecture based on cooperative processing and composed of different subsystems, each of them performing a specific task. These subsystems are:

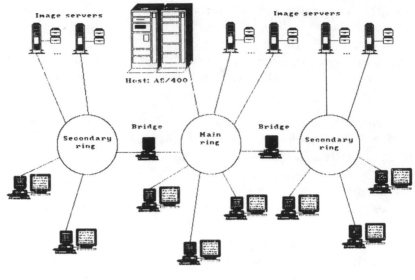

Fig. 1. Proposed LAN-based system architecture.

Textual Data Base
Visual Data
User Interface
Printing server
Communications

A scheme of the system is presented in Figure 1. The upper part of the figure corresponds to the true information system as described up to now, and the lower part shows another subsystem not listed above, the Image Acquisition component of the system, which is made up a set of stand-along digitizing work stations (off line with the information system).

In the final implementation of the AGI, the system might include up to 50 boxes (users' work stations and servers).

Conceptual Model

The subsystems are logic entities of the system architecture, more related to its required tasks than to the final implementation of such architecture. There is a middle step in the design process between the subsystems and its implementation, which is the Conceptual Model.

This model is composed of Functional Blocks, which are derived from the division of the subsystems' tasks in sets of logically related functions. The Functional Blocks run under Operational Environments, which are computers with its associated operating systems and communication facilities.

The conceptual model gives us the possibility of advancing in the design process with minimum machine dependence and, at the same time, allows us to change decisions on specific hardware to be used.

It is important to point out that, owing to the size of the archive and its related data bases, each of those Functional Blocks could run on a different computer (Operational Environment), or it will be possible to run all of them in a single machine, paving the way to use the system in much smaller archives.

Functional Blocks are listed below and are briefly described in the following paragraphs.

Communications subsystem
    Linking Interface
    Mail
User Interface2 subsystem
Textual Data Base subsystem
    Textual DB 1
    Textual DB 2
    Textual DB 3
Visual Data File subsystem
    Image Repository server
    Image Presentation
User's Management subsystem
    Access Control
    User's Data Base and System's Audit
Printing Server2 subsystem

Communications subsystem

Linking Interface. Every Functional Block has a symbolic name and communicates with other Functional Blocks sending asynchronous messages through a Functional Block called Linking Interface, which runs all the Operational Environments; its mission is, basically, to provide the rest of the Functional Blocks with the support needed for their dialogs.

As all the Functional Blocks could be running in the same Operational Environment or in different ones, the Linking Interface has to know at every moment the real configuration of the system and how to communicate with the different Operational Environments.

Other functions of the Linking Interface are:

Handling queues of incoming messages.
Detection of start and end of Functional Blocks.
Automatic rerouting to the Mail or messages addressed to inactive Functional Blocks.
Automatic presentation of messages existing in the Main, where a Functional Block starts.

Mail. This Functional Block is in charge of handling queues of those messages addressed to inactive Functional Blocks.

It is transparent for all the Functional Blocks except for the Linking Interface, which automatically reroutes to and retrieves from the Mail those messages.

User Interface2 subsystem

The User Interface runs in the user work stations and takes care of user dialog, converting user request into messages sent to other Functional Blocks and presenting the results answered back by them.

We are not making, at the design level, any assumption on how the user will initiate the action (keyboard, mouse, touch, or other way). This independence will allow us to adapt our design to get the most of new displays or input devices that might be available.

Every user action produces, after a dialogue asking for specific data if necessary, a message that is sent to the adequate Functional Block for its processing.

Despite the information's semantic variety, a unique formal format has been defined. This permits all the answers to the user's actions to be displayed by a single component: the Intelligent Browser.

Any operation implemented to be used with a specific type of information will be available on any information that the user wishes. With this design, the consistence of the man machine dialogue is guaranteed. Some of these operations are:

Specific object information and file print
Specific object information and file save for further use
Selective display of information
Different styles of presentation
Sort capabilities

The User Interface recognizes the type of user that it is dialoguing with and restricts the available functions accordingly. The types of users defined are:

Research
Archivist
Secretary
Administrator
Reading room controller

We are taking into account the latest developments in human factors. Different styles of window management and mouse interaction are under study.

Textual Data Base subsystem

Textual DB 1. It receives messages that define a user query on the archive inventory data base and ends up answering the identification of the objects satisfying the query.

Textual DB 2. It receives messages with identifiers of archive's objects and returns the existing information about them.

Textual DB 3. It receives messages with information related either to a new object to include in the data base, or to modifications of already existing objects, in order to maintain and update the information in the data base.

Visual Data File subsystem

Image Repository server. It controls the optical disk storage of document images (for example, juke-box). Receives messages with objects' id's and answers back with the images contained in them, typically manuscript pages or maps.

Image Presentation. The Image Presentation runs in the users' work stations and performs the display of the documents and maps. It also acts as a bridge between the User's Interface and the Image Repository server.

User's Management subsystem

Access Control. It controls the access of the users to the system and to the information contained in it.

User's Data Base and System's Audit. This functional block keeps information regarding users of the system, as well as the history of consulted documents.

Printing Server2 subsystem
The Printing Server handles the printers of the system.

Technical Aspects

In this chapter, some aspects related to the main servers of the system, mainly, the Textual Data Base and the Image Data File, are described.

Textual Data Base

This data base should contain all the information that is available today in the finding aids of the archive, and in those that will be available in the future. Therefore, the requirements are: (1) flexibility to be able to handle finding aids created along the archive history, updating and standardizing information created under different criteria and knowledge; and (2) ability to follow the basic principle that rules the archiving method—where the documents have come from. This reflects the structure of the hierarchy that holds the archive information (such as section, subsection, series, and sub-series).

Given these two main requirements, the information retrieval could be done by different methods: (1) classical free text search; (2) using descriptors originated by the staff of the Archive. A method will guide the user going from his key words to descriptors used by the archivist who cataloged the searched documents; (3) using queries following the hierarchy of the archive. The user could start at the top of the hierarchy and navigate through it by seeing the descendants of any object and its associated information. This type of interrogation will be mainly used with the top-level objects (sections, subsections, and series) and will be a replacement of the guide of the archive; (4) direct queries using signatures; or (5) queries bounded by dates.

In short, every unit of description, or object, will have the following data:

Signature
Short title
Data ranges
Descriptions
Descriptors

The descriptors could be qualified by their functions in the description unit to which they belong (such as sender, recipient, and king) and be related

TABLE 1
Estimated volumes for the Textual Data Base

Hypothesis	
• Number of objects in 1992	336,213
• Descriptor's average length	30
• Term's average length	10
• Description's average length	215
• Number of descriptors per object	5
• Number of terms per descriptor	3
• Number of descriptions per object	1
• Number of dates per object	1.5
• Average maximum level (hierarchy)	6
• Distinct terms (%)	20
• Distinct descriptors (%)	50

Note: Objects = sections, subsections, bundles, documents, plans, maps.

to other descriptors of the same document by specific relations (such as married to, father of, and sells to).

An additional function of the textual data base is to give a suitable link to the Visual Data File so that the appropriate document already digitized and stored in the Visual Data File could be retrieved and displayed on a screen.

The Textual Data Base will operate as a relational one using SQL (Structured Query Language) as the access tool. The minimum storage requirement to hold the available information, and the one generated in the near future, is estimated in 600 MB (million bytes). A detailed description of the volume of the information is shown in table 1.

Image Data File

Document processing

Introduction. The sizes of the documents stored in the archive vary from quarto (approximately half an A4 size) to big accounts bound books (35 × 55 cm), the largest part of them having old folio size (22 × 32 cm). This wide range has important implications for acquisition and storage and less important ones for visualization.

Archival documents do not have uniform background; sometimes the letters placed on one part of the document have more reflectance than the background of a different part. Also, preservation is occasionally bad, producing documents with almost broken letters, due to the ink type used; that is, the perimeter of each letter is cut, except in a few points. Any careless manipulation can destroy these letters.

Acquisition. Two different resolutions are being contemplated for the scanning of the documents. The first is 300 dots per inch (dpi) with only black and white information for documents similar to the ones handled in an office today. The second is 150 dpi with 16 levels of gray for the documents with subtle features and the degraded ones, thus requiring preprocessing before storing them in the final image storage media.

The acquisitions device must satisfy the requirements of safety. Thus, the selected scanners cannot use automatic document feeders.

Preprocessing. As is already known, archival documents lack uniform background. Our experiments show that some documents have significant background problems that prevent the use of standard scanning equipment. These systems assign only a black or white decision per image element (pixel), therefore storing one bit per pixel (1 bpp), this decision being the same for all of the document. Two different approaches can be considered to overcome this problem:

1. Scan at 1 bpp those documents that can be considered similar to the ones handled in the office environment.

2. Scan at 8 bpp (full gray-level range: 256 gray steps) the other documents and apply a preprocessing stage to reduce that amplitude to 1 bpp afterward. Segmentation with variable threshold decision based on a multistage evaluation of the background will be applied, the problems being the high number of operations required. To solve it, we are exploring the use of special hardware accelerators.

Storage. To estimate the required storage, let us consider that the average image size is slightly higher than A4, giving 12 million points at 300 dpi. Then a document will require 1.5 MB (B stands for a byte, or 8 bits) before compression and, with a 1/12 compression ratio, 130 KB for the compressed data. For the documents digitized in gray levels, 3 MB of storage are required to store one page. If we assume a compression ratio of 3 for multilevel images, the compressed data will occupy 1 MB per page.

As we have said earlier, the only way of handling this huge amount of information is use of optical storage. Currently, there are optical disks with a capacity of 10 GB. About 117 of them will be required to store, when digitized in binary form, the target set of 9 million pages.

Visualization. Our experience indicates that the complete width of a written document must be displayed at the same time to avoid uncomfortable left and right displacements for every line. The same does not hold for the vertical dimension because there is no problem to scroll up and down.

Map processing

Introduction. The number of elements included in the section of Maps and Drawings is 7,000, one half of them being pure maps. The other half corresponds to special items that cannot be included with the documents such as cloths, stamps, and nonpaper documents.

Map sizes have a large range of values. Big maps are almost 2 square meters in size. Small ones do not reach 0.02 square meters. Therefore, there is a 1 to 100 ratio. The average map is about 80 × 70 cm.

The use of color is employed in most of them, usually to mark specific areas of the map. The monochrome version (photocopy) has the main information.

Acquisition. The resolution to scan the maps is governed by the smallest letter found in them. We are now considering digitizing at least at 4 points per millimeter (4 ppmm). For the average map, it gives 3,200 × 2,800 pixels.

The common characteristic of all elements included in map selection is that they must be digitized using a multilevel scheme. Depending on the chrome, a one byte per pixel approach will be used for gray images (256 levels) and a two byte per pixel for color images (32 levels for each color).

Using CDD cameras, we can obtain images with 4,470 × 3,450 pixels, which with the previous resolution represent surfaces of 1.12 × 0.85 m.

Storage. The objective is to keep the monochrome maps compressed to 2 bpp, thus requiring the use of lossy encoding techniques. The current approach is to use hierarchical encoding schemes to allow for the display of gross resolution versions of the map. The color maps should be compressed to 3 bpp.

If we assume that half the maps are monochrome and the other half color, an average of 2.5 bpp is obtained. As the average map is 3,200 × 2,800 pixels, the required storage is 2.7 MB. Therefore the total number of maps need 18.7 GB, which fits into two optical disks.

If no compression is applied, an average of 12 bpp is obtained. The average map requires 12.8 MB. The total number of maps needs 87.7 GB; therefore, they can be stored in nine optical disks. This analysis shows that the compression of maps is not a negative point in the feasibility of the system.

Furthermore, the hierarchical organization of the data provides an appealing approach to deal with browsing and with different resolutions.

Visualization Color image displays with higher resolution than 1,024 × 1,024 based on PCs do not seem close at hand. The present approach is to operate with a 1,024 × 1,024 display that does not hold a full average map (3,200 × 2,800), but that is enough to handle a decimated version of it. One-quarter of the resolution requires 800 × 700, which is smaller than the display size. The full resolution will be supported by screening parts of the map.

Cooperation frame

The cooperation frame is described in a protocol signed by the three parties.

The Ministry of Culture will be responsible for the organization of the work in the archive, the site preparation, the enhancement of the description of the records, and the normalization that will allow the extension to other archives.

The expenses of hardware acquisition, system development, personnel training, and the loading of the data base will be covered by the Ramón Areces Foundation and IBM Spain.

All the parties will be responsible for the functional design of the system.

Appendix A: Two examples of the General Archive of the Indies

The operations performed to obtain the reproductions were the following:

Ratification of the testament of Columbus, 1506 (figure 2):
1. Digitization of the original at 100 dpi using Xerox 7650 scanner.
2. Processing of selected areas of the document to increase their legibility (upper part: contrast enhancement; lower part: background uniformization). The operations were done in an IBM PS/2 model 70.
3. Printing at 300 dpi using an IBM 4216 laser printer.

City plan of Panama, 1673 (figure 3):
1. Digitization of a microfilm at 40 microns/pixel using a Perkin-Elmer 101A microdensitometer.
2. Color dithering using error diffusion.
3. Printing at 135 dpi using an IBM 5087 color printer.

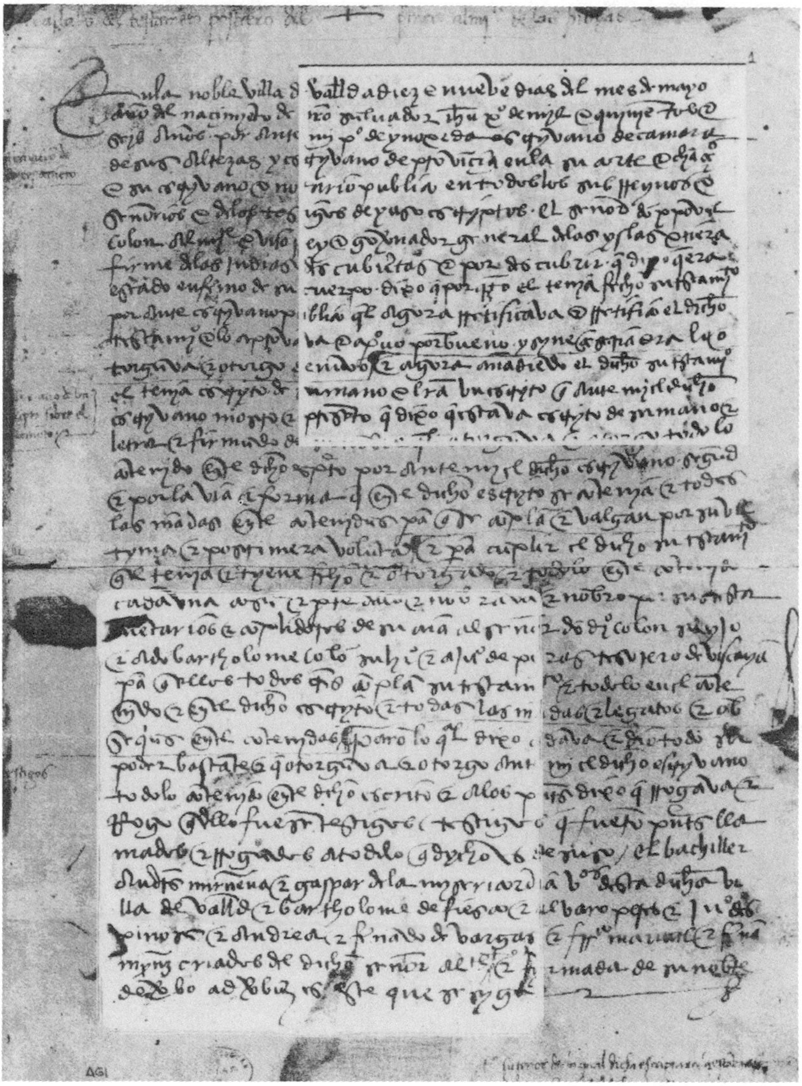

Fig. 2. The ratification of the testament of Columbus.

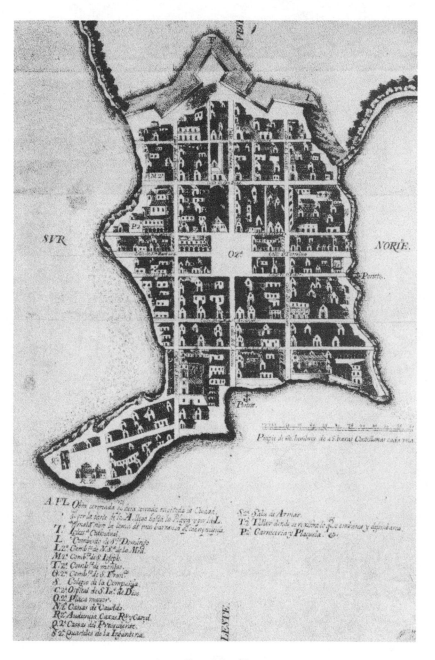

Fig. 3. City plan of Panama.

Appendix B: Current status of the project (August 1990)

Digitization

This part of the project was started in 1988. Since then, around 2 million pages have been captured and stored in optical disks. Digitization of more documents is being performed now at a rate of around 250,000 pages/month. This implies that by the end of 1992 about 8.5 million pages will be stored in the picture data base.

The process of digitization implies three different stages: bundle sorting, document capture, and verification (quality control). IBM Personal System/2 computers are being used for the latter two tasks.

Thirty people are currently working in document capture. Another ten persons are performing bundle sorting.

Loading of the textual data base

Around 80 percent of the Textual Data Base has already been loaded in an IBM AS/400 computer. There are ten people doing this work, which was started in 1987.

Development of the system. A prototype of the final system has been developed and is operating at the archive at Seville. This system is comprised of an AS/400 (Textual Data Base, User's Management subsystem), and Personal System/2's with high resolution monochrome monitors (users' work stations, Image Servers). Everything is connected through an IBM Token Ring.

Using the system, the users can make queries to the Textual Data Base, access images of the documents, process them, manipulate them, and so forth.

Although this prototype is still limited, new functions are being added and, as they are finished, incorporated at the system at Seville.

The next step in the development will be to include a map capture and visualization system (in color). This task has already begun and will be finished shortly. The access to the images will be carried out using PS/2 and high-resolution color displays.

The development team is composed of twenty persons.

NOTE

1. Document elaborated by the project working group (April 1988).

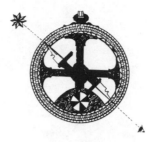

5 · Recommendations

Introduction to Part 5

John TePaske casts an eye backward, in contrast to Becerril and his colleagues' look into the future. TePaske has been involved at many stages in the continuing preparations to produce a guide to Hispanic and Latin American manuscript collections in the United States, and his review of the somewhat striated history of that project—which dates back more than thirty years to 1960—provides us with a clear view of what has come and with a call to complete the project as part of this country's Quincentennial commemoration.

JOHN JAY TEPASKE

16. A History and Personal Memoir of the Project to Prepare a Guide to Latin American Source Materials in the United States

The project to develop a guide to Hispanic American manuscripts held in repositories in the United States has had a checkered history. After an auspicious beginning in the 1960s, the project languished. Efforts to revive it, some feeble and some strong, were made in the 1970s and 1980s. This book is another episode in the saga. More than one contributor to it has been involved in fashioning the project at one time or another. He/she will share not only my sense of déja vu but also, I hope, an optimism that this time concrete action will result.

The guide project began in 1959 in Paris at the International Council of Archives. There the delegates recommended preparation of guides to the historical sources for Latin America housed in repositories in Europe, the United States, and Australia. In 1960, under the aegis of the Hispanic Division of the Library of Congress, a commission was organized to initiate and conduct a survey of the repositories containing Latin American materials in the United States. The Rockefeller Foundation provided funds for defraying the costs of planning the project. The advisory committee, which met in December 1963, was chaired by Theodore R. Schellenberg and consisted of Nettie Lee Benson, Howard Cline, Lewis Hanke, John P. Harrison, Gunnar Mendoza, and George S. Ulibarri. At that meeting Schellenberg and Mendoza, who had agreed to be director and principal investigator for the project, outlined the specific guidelines, methods, and procedures to be used. The advisory committee made specific suggestions on the proposals presented by Schellenberg and Mendoza. Among the guidelines established in 1963, which might be of interest to this group, were that geographical coverage was to include all Latin American nations and Puerto Rico (to 1898). The Philippine islands, former Spanish possessions now part of the United States, and the non-Spanish Caribbean were to be excluded. Except for scrapbooks, clippings, and the like, printed materials were not to be included in the guide. Collections of documents inaccessible for research were also to be excluded, unless they were being made available in the near future. The committee recommended no chronological limits for the project. The primary language was to be English.

Sponsored by the Society of American Archivists and the Hispanic Foundation of the Library of Congress and with funding from the Institute of Latin American Studies at the University of Texas and the Rockefeller Foundation, the project moved forward with gusto under the able direction of Dr. Mendoza, who with the aid of two assistants began to develop the guide entries. By the fall of 1967 Mendoza and his associates had compiled a listing of 5,820 collections and descriptions of some 1,500 of them, 400 supplementary lists of reference sources, 800 inquiries to United States repositories, and listings of 404 with Latin American materials. All this is testimony to the hard work and indefatigability of Gunnar Mendoza, whom many of you know as one of the best qualified archivists in all Latin America. Needed to round out the guide in the fall of 1967 were the completion of some 3,500 descriptive entries, visits to some of the principal repositories with Latin American materials where information provided was incomplete, preparation of a general introduction and index for the guide, general editing of the manuscript, and preparation of a card file for the guide to be kept permanently at the University of Texas Institute for Latin American Studies. In 1967 the Council of Library Resources made $18,000 available for completion of the project, but NEH denied a grant request for a bit over $30,000 for the same purpose. For whatever reasons, Mendoza went home to Bolivia, and the Council on Library Resources withdrew its support for the project. Except for the movement of the Mendoza files to a new building at the University of Texas, the project languished. Mendoza resumed his archival duties in Bolivia and as a consultant for UNESCO; the advisory committee fell into desuetude, I assume because of the deaths of Theodore Schellenberg and Howard Cline; and nothing was done to maintain the momentum that Mendoza had established between 1963 and 1967.

Six years later in March 1973, Mendoza himself stimulated renewed interest in the project. In a visit to the Library of Congress he pessimistically reported to the director of the Latin American, Spanish, and Portuguese

Division that there was a great deal more to the project than he had envisioned originally. New acquisitions by various repositories now made it necessary to update his previous entries. Unlike his view six years before that it would take only a year to complete the guide, he now believed two years were necessary. He also suggested that replacements were needed on the advisory committee for Schellenberg and Cline. The impression one gets from the report of this meeting is that Mendoza left for Bolivia in the spring of 1973 very pessimistic about the future of the project.

One result of Mendoza's visit, however, was to spur a new meeting of the advisory committee, which, as far as I can determine, had not met in ten years. On November 17, 1973, the group reconvened at the Library of Congress. On a positive note the advisory committee expanded its membership to include a representative from the Seminar for the Acquisition of Latin American Library Materials (SALALM). Also, a representative from the University of Texas expressed an interest in seeing the project through, suggesting that Stanley Ross be added to the advisory committee and that William Glade be contacted to give impetus to fund raising for the project. As far as can be determined, Ross and Glade were not added to the advisory committee, nor did the University of Texas pursue its efforts to obtain funding for the guide project.

Three years later, on October 2, 1976, the committee met again at the Library of Congress. After a careful review of the project and developments that had occurred since 1967, it was decided that at least three years would now be needed to complete the project. Nettie Lee Benson offered space at the University of Texas and a generous amount of her own time as a possible director for the project. As chair of the Conference on Latin American History (CLAH) Stanley Stein gave his enthusiastic endorsement of the project, and Mary E. Kahler of the Library of Congress was to look into possibilities for funding. Lewis Hanke attempted to shame the committee into more vigorous action by displaying the guides published for Spain and the British Isles, which fulfilled the commitment made in 1959 at the Paris meeting of the International Council on Archives. As always, a lively discussion of what the guide should include and how it should be updated ensued. The result of all this was a new grant proposal to NEH by the University of Texas for a three-year subvention to complete the project. It was not funded by NEH.

In February 1980, the project got new life from the new chief of the Hispanic Division of the Library of Congress, William Carter. I also became involved personally for the first time. Carter's desire to promote the project seems to have stemmed from a number of factors: first was his strong feeling that the project was worthwhile and would result in an exceedingly valuable research tool that should be supported vigorously by his division and by him as the new chief; second, encouraging the project went hand-in-hand with similar projects being carried on at the Library of Congress for which the new computer technology was ideally suited; and third, he had received discreet inquiries from the National Endowment for the Humanities about the fate of the guide project. It appears that the endowment was being presented with an increasing number of grant requests from American repositories for projects involving the cataloging or calendaring of their Hispanic American source materials. Without the guide, endowment officials were finding it increasingly difficult to determine the utility, desirability, or value of the grant proposals coming across their desks. Carter thus invited three members of CLAH to Washington in February 1980 to draft a proposal for a workshop to revive the project. That proposal was subsequently funded by NEH.

The workshop took place in late January 1981. There were twenty-six participants, representing archivists, librarians, administrators, and historians, as well as a number of observers. The participants presented formal papers. Except for one question—Should this be a new project?—the workshop posed the same questions with which previous advisory committees had grappled: What constitutes Hispanic American? How should *manuscript* be defined? What should be the structure of guide entries? Should the project be open-ended? Could it combine a finite product with a long-range program? Should the project cover all repositories? Should the guide include copied material? If priorities are set up, what should they be? What should be the temporal and geographical limits of the guide? Following the workshop, Tom Niehaus, Lawrence Clayton, Murdo MacLeod, William Carter, and John Hébert drafted a final report. John TePaske edited it with the help of William Carter and prepared it for distribution to approximately one hundred institutions and individuals.

The workshop made the following recommendations.

1. The American Historical Association (AHA), with the affiliation of CLAH, should be given the responsibility for sponsoring and carrying out the project. The Library of Congress should house the project.

2. The Council of the AHA should appoint an advisory group for the project. This group should include representatives from AHA and CLAH

and professional groups of librarians and archivists, scholars in other relevant fields, and the Hispanic American community in the United States.

3. The project should begin with a survey of repositories in the United States that contain Latin American manuscripts or archives. The survey should follow the format used by RLIN (American Research Libraries Information Network), to which NUCMC (National Union Catalog of Manuscript Collections) is now conforming, and should include directory information such as the name of the repository, address, and hours of operation. It should also include a brief description of its manuscript and archival collections and a list of available finding aids. The survey should include all types of repositories and be as comprehensive as possible. Preservation needs should be addressed.

4. The project should make use of pertinent information already gathered to produce the guide, such as the Gunnar Mendoza files and the ongoing survey of the Library of Congress.

5. The information obtained from the survey should be placed in the archival format developed by RLIN.

6. The project should use the information from the survey of repositories as a first step in producing the guide. The initial survey should act as a skeleton to which will be added more detailed information about the collections themselves in order to produce the guide.

7. The types of repositories included in the project should be federal and international archives and libraries in the United States, state and local archives, university and research institution archives, corporate archives, and any other repositories in the United States containing Latin American manuscripts and archives.

8. The guide to the collections should not repeat detailed descriptions published elsewhere but should include a reference to those descriptions. In the case of previously undescribed collections, it should give a more detailed description but still a brief one.

9. Every effort should be made to include in the guide, manuscript collections and archives relating to the history of Hispanic Americans, as long as the dates of these collections fall within the limitations set by the advisory board.

10. The advisory board should seek funding for the project from a broad range of sources. This includes the National Endowment for the Humanities and other agencies as well as possible matching funds from some corporations whose collections may be included in the guide.

11. The National Union Catalog of Manuscript Collections should be given sufficient financial support from its funding source to enable it to automate its operation, so vital to the needs of the scholarly community as a possible automated vehicle for future updating of the proposed guide to Latin American manuscript collections.

Because I was chairman of CLAH the year those recommendations were made, which was also the reason for my involvement in 1980, they weighed heavily on me. I thus spent most of the spring and summer of 1981 seeking out an advisory committee, drafting a grant proposal to NEH, and generally following the dictates of the January workshop. I should mention here that I did not act alone; I had the aid and support of a great number of people from CLAH and elsewhere. Unfortunately, however, in my position as chair of CLAH, I could not elicit support from the University of Texas for a joint proposal. CLAH unilaterally sent forward a three-year grant proposal to NEH for the guide project that was ultimately rejected, primarily on the grounds that it closely resembled a similar proposal put forward at the same time by the University of Texas. NEH instructed CLAH and the University of Texas to resubmit a proposal that *both* supported. This was done. My successor as chairman of CLAH, Herbert S. Klein, with Larry Clayton and others, was successful in hammering out a joint proposal with the University of Texas to do a guide to Latin American manuscripts in the United States, a proposal most of us believed would receive support. Going forward in August 1982, the grant request provided for a three-year project situated the first year at the University of Texas and the last two in Washington, D.C. The first year was to be spent putting the Mendoza entries into machine-readable form. The remaining two years were to be used for updating and expanding the guide and getting it ready for publication. That project was not funded. Although I was not privy to the critiques, I believe it was turned down mostly for the way in which the entries were to be put into machine-readable form. Klein called me about the rejection; so too did Tom Davies, executive secretary of CLAH. We all agreed that CLAH had done its best, that we had given the project enough of our time and energy, and that we should lay the proposal to rest once and for all.

The matter may have ended here for many of us, but in the fall of 1986 James Gardner at the AHA called me to say that there was an effort being made to institute a guide project to identify collections of Latin American manuscripts in the United States. My reaction was somewhere between shock and amusement; a new guide project redux, redux, redux? This brings us to the present. My hope is that this brief history of this project to 1987 combined with the personal memoir will keep us from repeating the errors of the past, that the enthusiasm and impetus of the Quintocentenario will generate the money, time, and effort to get a guide finally into a usable form. I can think of few contributions that would be as useful and valuable—or as fitting—to commemorate the five hundredth anniversary of the discovery of the New World.

LAWRENCE A. CLAYTON

Conclusion
Formal Recommendations to the Conference

Results and Recommendations Arising from the Conference
on Hispanic Archives and Records for the Study of the
Hispanic Experience in the United States, 1492–1850,
Library of Congress, September 22–25, 1987

1. The conference unanimously recommended that its proceedings be published in an appropriate fashion, with an introduction and inclusion of the recommendations and resolutions of the conference.

2. On the copying aspect of the project (the principal theme of this conference), it was agreed that until a thorough survey of Hispanic source materials for the study of Latin America and the Hispanic presence in North America be completed, it would be difficult to proceed with a major or master copying project abroad to fill in those collections in the United States that contain materials for the study of the Hispanic experience in the United States.

While several such valuable projects were described at this conference—Hoffman'a report on Louisiana, Gannon and Lyon's report on Florida, Kessell's report on the Vargas Project, New Mexico, and others—the conference agreed that the production of a Guide to Hispanic Manuscripts and Collections in the United States be the principal goal. This would integrate the copying project(s) related to the Hispanic experience in the United States into the long-range plans, as a second, third, or fourth stage.

3. An Advisory Committee of the Guide to Hispanic Manuscripts in the United States Project was then appointed:

Lawrence Clayton, History, Alabama (Chairman)
David Block, Library Science, Cornell

Mark Burkholder, History, Missouri, St. Louis
Kathleen Deagan, Anthropology, Florida
David Gracy, Archives, Texas
Laura Gutiérrez-Witt, Library Science, Texas
Paul Hoffman, History, Louisiana State University
Thomas Niehaus, Library Science, Tulane
Guadalupe Jiménez-Codinach, Hispanic Division, Library of Congress
Helen Nader, ex-officio, chairman of the American Historical Association Columbus Quincentenary Committee
John Hébert, ex-officio, acting chief of the Hispanic Division, Library of Congress
James Gardner, ex-officio, deputy executive director, American Historical Association
John Russell-Wood, ex-officio, chairman of the Conference on Latin American History Columbus Quincentenary Committee

4. David Block and Thomas Niehaus volunteered to produce a first draft of a grant proposal to the NEH to commence the guide project. This would essentially be an updated and revised proposal of the one submitted by CLAH and the University of Texas in 1982. It was also generally agreed that the copying of manuscripts abroad for the Hispanic experience in the United States be part of the project, even if proposed only in the long range or as a second or third stage to the project.

5. The committee agreed that the general administrative structure most appropriate to the long-range project be modeled on that used in the Guide to Historical Literature (3rd edition) project currently being sponsored by the American Historical Association. In this project, John Higham of Johns Hopkins will be the general editor and act in an overall executive administrative role. Higham will receive approximately one-quarter time for his general editorship. The actual project will be housed at the University of Maryland, College Park, and will have a full-time editor who will organize fifty-five section editors across the country. The publisher will be Oxford University Press. Although our guide project need not be a mirror image, the Guide to Historical Literature does appear to be an excellent model.

6. The committee recommended that much of the actual surveying work involved in describing the contents of those collections to be included in the guide be done at the local, state, and regional levels wherever those best equipped to do so may reside. We should push for voluntary contributions

in time and work and for the reshuffling of priorities in local, state, and regional depositories to help the project share the costs and responsibilities. Nonetheless, funds should be made available through the guide project budget to reimburse expenses and compensate for work done at the local, state, or regional levels that cannot be accomplished by contributions of work in kind. State humanities councils, national and regionally oriented professional organizations, and other such groups were identified as important possible contributors to the cost- and labor-sharing dimension of the project.

7. It was agreed that the project should be a long-term one to describe the collections with brief, but adequate, scope and content notes and to provide for a continuous updating in the future, patterned roughly on such ongoing activities as the National Union Catalog of Manuscript Collections and the Handbook of Latin American Studies. The committee recognized that large expenses (see item 8) will be incurred over the years in the project and recommended that it be stepped, or achieved in stages. It was also generally agreed— although with some debate—that a preliminary, general description of collections and materials be made available as soon as possible, perhaps as soon as eighteen months after the funding and initiation of the project. The users group was the most vocal in wanting this preliminary guide. Tom Niehaus of Tulane, who prepared a detailed report of the conference's recommendations that paralleled this one in most respects, reported more specifically that "the historians (users group) want a preliminary report of information gathered after 18 months, being mostly the already existing information provided by the repositories. This preliminary report is seen as a loose-leaf list that could be updated. They suggest that it include original manuscripts, copies, transcripts, and archaeological collections. The librarians, archivists and some other historians (providers group and methods group) felt that the preliminary information wanted by the users group could be provided as print outs or other provisional publications made from the data base."

8. It was agreed that a project whose budget may exceed $500,000 and, in fact, go over a million dollars in the course of its lifetime could not—would not—be funded in whole by any one institution such as the NEH. It was thus recommended that efforts be initiated soon to develop fund raising through such organizations as the AHA and the Columbus Jubilee Quincentenary Commission. The commission should be asked for their formal sponsorship of this project.

9. It was agreed that the Research Libraries Information Network (RLIN)

format of manuscript description be adopted for the project. It is rapidly becoming the standard format, is about to be adopted by NUCMC, and is an on-line data system that lends itself to ease of updating, retrieval, and communications, while hard copies (printed editions) can be made with facility.

10. The committee recommended that the AHA be the principal sponsoring institution, and the AHA's representative (Jim Gardner) agreed to present the project before the AHA Executive Committee, which convenes in December and must formally approve AHA sponsorship. The Conference on Latin American History (CLAH) would be affiliated with the project as a cosponsoring institution, but the AHA will be the principal promoter and director of the project. Presumably other organizations such as professional organizations of librarians, archivists, anthropologists, and the like might be asked to join any major grant raising effort as cosponsors.

Other items that were discussed:
BITNET as the principal communications network.
Staging of application(s) to NEH.
More specific fund-raising suggestions.

NOTE: Since the above recommendations were made and reviewed by the committee appointed at the end of the conference (see item 3 above), details of the project have changed, but the goals have not. The American Historical Association applied directly in 1991 to the National Endowment for the Humanities for a major grant entitled "Improving Access to Latin American and Hispanic Materials in the U.S." to produce a guide to Hispanic manuscripts and collections in the United States. Professor John F. Schwaller of Florida Atlantic University is directing this effort. Meanwhile, the Hispanic Division of the Library of Congress has completed its production of a guide to copies of Hispanic manuscripts and collections in the United States.

The publication of these proceedings is the first step in the overall project that the AHA and the LC, in cooperation with the Conference on Latin American History, the Ohio State University Press, and the University of Florida, hope to complete by 1996.

Contributors

José Luis Becerril is director of the IBM Scientific Center, Madrid, Spain.

Lawrence A. Clayton is Professor of History and was director of the Latin American Studies Program at the University of Alabama, Tuscaloosa.

William S. Coker is Professor of History and chairman of the Department of History, University of West Florida, Pensacola.

Michael V. Gannon is Professor of History and director of the Institute for Early Contact Period Studies at the University of Florida, Gainesville.

Pedro González is director of the Center for Archival Documentary Information, Ministry of Culture, Madrid.

Laura Gutiérrez-Witt is director of the Nettie Lee Benson Latin American Collection at the University of Texas, Austin.

Paul E. Hoffman is Professor of History, Louisiana State University, Baton Rouge.

Charles Hudson is Professor of Anthropology, University of Georgia, Athens.

Guadalupe Jiménez-Codinach is with the Hispanic Division, Library of Congress, Washington, D.C.

Douglas E. Jones is director of the University of Alabama Museums, Tuscaloosa.

John L. Kessell is Associate Professor of History and editor of the Vargas Project at the University of New Mexico, Albuquerque.

Miguel Latasa is with the Ramón Areces Foundation, Madrid, Spain.

Eugene Lyon is director of the Center for Historic Research, St. Augustine Foundation, Flagler College, St. Augustine, Florida.

Harriet Ostroff is editor of the National Union Catalog of Manuscript Collections, Library of Congress, Washington, D.C.

Charles W. Polzer, S.J., is curator of ethnohistory, Arizona State Museum, University of Arizona, Phoenix.

Michael C. Scardaville is Professor of History and director of the Latin American Studies Program, University of South Carolina, Columbia.

John Jay TePaske is Professor of History, Duke University, Durham, North Carolina.

Margarita Vázquez de Parga is with the Ministry of Culture in Madrid, Spain.

Alan Virta is head of special collections, Boise State University Library, Idaho.

Index